Helion & Company Limited
Unit 8 Amherst Business Centre
Budbrooke Road
Warwick
CV34 5WE
England
Tel. 01926 499 619
Email: info@helion.co.uk
Website: www.helion.co.uk
Twitter: @helionbooks

Original edition co-published by Helion &
Company Limited and 30° South Publishers
(Pty) Limited 2011. This revised edition
published by Helion & Company Limited
2019

This edition incorporates elements designed
and typeset by 30° South Publishers (Pty)
Limited. Additional typesetting by Farr out
Publications, Wokingham, Berkshire
Cover designed by Paul Hewitt, Battlefield
Design (www.battlefield-design.co.uk)

Text © Peter Baxter 2011
Colour aviation profiles © Tom Cooper 2019
Colour vehicle profiles © David Bocquelet
      2019

ISBN 978-1-912866-89-2

British Library Cataloguing-in-Publication
Data.
A catalogue record for this book is available
from the British Library.

For details of other military history titles
published by Helion & Company Limited
contact the above address, or visit our
website: http://www.helion.co.uk.

We always welcome receiving book
proposals from prospective authors.

CONTENTS

GLOSSARY

ABA	AB Aerotransport	MCD	Marine Commando Division
AHQ	Army Headquarters	NCNC	National Council of Nigerian Citizens
ANC	*Armée Nationale Congolaise*	NCO	non-commissioned officer
ARMSCOR	Armaments Corporation of South Africa	NNS	Nigerian Navy Service
BBC	British Broadcasting Corporation	NPC	Northern People's Congress
BOFF	Biafran Organization of Freedom Fighters	OAS	*Organisation de l'Armée Secrète*
BP	British Petroleum	OAU	Organization of African Unity
CIO	Central Intelligence Organization	RAF	Royal Air Force
DHQ	Divisional Headquarters	RPG	rocket-propelled grenade
GOC	General Officer Commanding	RWAFF	Royal West Africa Frontier Force
HQ	Headquarters	SDECE	*Service de Documentation Extérieure et de Contre-Espionnage*
ICRC	International Committee of the Red Cross		
LGO	Lagos Garrison Organization	UDI	unilateral declaration of independence

INTRODUCTION

But we were reading Arabic for centuries while they were still cannibals ...
— *New York Times,* 13 December 1966

Nigerian writer Chinua Achebe, in his personal memoir of the Biafran conflict, *There Was A Country*, made an unusually candid admission in relation to the Nigerian colonial experience.

Here is a piece of heresy. The British governed their colony of Nigeria with considerable care. There was a very highly competent cadre of government officials imbued with a high level of knowledge of how to run a country. This was not something that the British achieved only in Nigeria; they were able to manage this on a bigger scale in India and Australia. The British had the experience of governing and doing it competently. I am not justifying colonialism. But it is important to face the fact that British colonies, more or less, were expertly run.[1]

Heresy indeed, but there is a great deal of truth in this comment nonetheless. The British Colonial Service was a professional corps of bureaucrats and administrators of an extremely high calibre. Bearing in mind how thinly spread across the imperial spectrum the good men were, it was an impressive achievement that the British Empire at its peak was as expertly and moderately managed as it was. Nigeria, however, was particularly gifted in having the attentions at a crucial period in its evolution of Sir Frederick Lugard.*

Chinua Achebe. *Source NNDB*

Sir Frederick Lugard.

Sir Harry Johnston.

Sir William Milton.

---

* The Colonial Service was unified in the 1930s. Prior to this, applications and appointments were on a territorial basis and required an application directed to an individual territorial bureaucracy. Governorships and viceregal appointments were made through the Colonial Office. After the 1930s a unified Colonial Service existed, comprising 16 sub-services, with each officer a member of both the appropriate sub-service of the Colonial Service and of the civil service of the territory in which he served.

Lugard ranks among a handful of exceptional administrators active in Africa during the last decade of the 19th century and the first decade of the 20th century. Sir Harry Johnston was another of these, a man of diminutive stature but colossal wit and gumption who was instrumental in the evolution of Nyasaland into a crown protectorate. Yet another was William Milton, who almost

The Kabul Gate in the city wall of Jellalabad, the Second Afghan War, 1878–80. *Source Private Collection*

The British Army camp at Fort Jamrud, Afghanistan, 1879. *Source Private Collection*

The Battle of El Teb during the Sudanese Campaign, 1884. *Sketch Melton Prior*

The surrender of the Burmese Army in the Third Anglo-Burmese War, 27 November 1885.

single-handedly created the executive, judicial and administrative infrastructure of Rhodesia, what would later be Zimbabwe. And then of course, there was Lugard himself.

Lugard was a sparse, rather ascetic individual. Short, highbrowed, with deep set eyes, an intense and penetrating stare, his only apparent concession to vanity was a long and finely tapered moustache that varied in volume and length during the phases of his life. He was, at his core, a military man, with a soldier's uncluttered perspective and finely tuned sense of duty. Son of an army chaplin, Lugard was born in India, where he later served with the 2nd Battalion the 9th Regiment of Foot, which in 1881 became the East Norfolk Regiment. He saw action in the 1878–80 Second Afghan War, during the Sudanese Campaign of 1884 and the Third Burmese War of 1885. He was instrumental in the final defeat of slavery in Nyasaland and the Lakes region, and in the acquisition for the British Crown of the territories of Uganda.

It is for his work in Nigeria, though, that Lugard is perhaps best known. His first deployment to the region was in 1898 to oversee the formation of the Royal West African Frontier Force. The RWAFF was an interesting formation, created as an amalgamation of all British colonial military forces in West Africa, with battalions drawn from each substantive British West African territory. It was a largely native military force established to secure the borders of

British West Africa against French imperial and economic intrusion, and later to secure and pacify the various territories and regions that would in due course comprise the British territory of Nigeria. It grew ultimately into an orthodox, British-style military formation that saw action in both the First and Second World Wars, in both cases in Africa, but also in Burma during the Second World War.

In Nigeria the RWAFF comprised two divisions, north and south, which was an early concession to something of a cultural gulf that existed between the Islamized north and the traditional/animist south. The first force raised was northern. These the British grouped together as Hausa. Hausa thereafter became the *lingua franca* of the force, and for some time it was the *lingua franca* of RWAFF as a whole, remaining so in fact until the end of colonial rule.

West Africa was largely of greater economic and global strategic interest to the British than as a potential settled British colony along the lines of Kenya, South Africa or Rhodesia. Conditions tended to be hostile to white settlement, and so those expatriates resident in the region, in territories as diverse as The Gambia, Sierra Leone, Gold Coast and Nigeria, were thus on the whole engaged either in the administration and defence of the territory, or engaged in business. The region was not settled in any meaningful way by Europeans, and indeed very few Europeans

Gold Coast military forces, the Royal West African Frontier Force. *Source Private Collection*

Sir George Dashwood Taubman Goldie. *Source Private Collection*

British Liberal prime minister, William Gladstone.

remained behind in the various territories once independence had been granted.

The modern history of the West African region as a whole, in particular in relation to the activities of all its various European interlopers, tended to be informed in large part by the slave trade, which of course concurred with the development and industrialization of the plantation economies of the Americas. During this period European involvement consisted of little more than highly organized plunder. It was aggressive, destructive and lucrative, but also manifestly unsustainable. Toward the middle of the 1800s, therefore, the complexion of business in the region began to alter, with a tendency toward more infrastructure-dependent and sustainable systems of commerce. This in turn required organization, management and security, which at the time were all supplied by the Royal Niger Company, a royal chartered company chaired by one of the great Victorian capitalists, Sir George Taubman Goldie.

Goldie, the gifted son of a substantial Manx military officer and politician, travelled extensively in Africa as a young man. During a visit to West Africa in 1877 he accurately concluded that the Niger Delta and its hinterland would offer rich commercial opportunity to any crown or organization that cared to claim it. At that time the British government, led alternately by Liberal prime minister William Gladstone and Conservative prime minister Benjamin Disraeli, had a very limited appetite for the expense or responsibility of annexing new territory in Africa, or anywhere else for that matter. At precisely the same time more abstract men like Victorian aesthete and social thinker John Ruskin were espousing the divine right of Britannia to rule, and urging the empire's worthiest and most energetic sons, such as Goldie himself, to take to the field in furtherance of the glory of the Crown.

John Ruskin (8 February 1819– 20 January 1900) was an English author, poet and artist, although more famous for his work as an art and social critic. Ruskin's thinking on art and architecture became the thinking of the Victorian and Edwardian eras.

Those sons of England inclined to respond were often forced to do so on the back of private capital, and in order to consolidate the diverse British business interests already established in the Delta region, Goldie formed the United Africa Company, later the National Africa Company, which was floated in 1879 on a capital subscription of £1 million, and which received a royal charter in 1888. The National Africa Company invested heavily in the Delta region, developing a comprehensive river transport system that effectively check-mated French entrepreneurs and imperialists who were concurrently trying to gain a foothold in the region. Thus, during 1884–5 when the Berlin Conference was convened to map out European spheres of influence in Africa, and thanks largely to Goldie's own efforts, Britain was in a position to claim an almost *de facto* annexation of the Niger Delta region, and quite a large swath of what was at that time still referred to on international shipping charts as the Slave Coast.

With an imprimatur in hand to pacify and govern, legalized by its royal charter, the National Africa Company became the Royal Niger Company, and the era of modern Nigeria was born. The coast and the northern reaches of the territory were declared separate British protectorates under Company administration, with the British imperial government itself only assuming control of the combined Niger territories in 1900, after which, in 1914, the two entities merged to form the Colony and Protectorate of Nigeria.

British Conservation prime minister, Benjamin Disraeli.

Three of the five British aircraft carriers involved in the Suez operation: HMS *Eagle* (R05) leads HMS *Bulwark* (R08) and HMS *Albion* (R07). *Source Private Collection*

A British Centurion tank of the 6th Royal Tank Regiment disembarks from the tank-landing ship HMS *Puncher* (L3036) at Port Said. In the background can be seen the De Lesseps statue which stood at the entrance to the Suez Canal, 1956. *Source Private Collection*

The first British governor of a united Nigeria was none other than Sir Frederick Lugard. Prior to this, between 1900 and 1906, Lugard had served as governor of the northern protectorate and had already cultivated his much-storied admiration for the aristocratic emirs and the northern Sokoto Caliphate that continued to exist at that time as a governing paramountcy. At that time Lugard happened to be married to the highly influential newspaper columnist and social commentator Flora Shaw, and it would be instructive here to quote from one or two of her and Lord Lugard's many acclamations on the peoples of northern Nigeria, just to give an indication of how in awe she and her husband both were of these ancient people of the Sahel. According to Lady Lugard: *

> The Fulani were a striking people, dark in complexion, but of the distinguished features, small hands, and fine, rather aristocratic carriage of the Arabs on the Mediterranean coast. They were of the Mahomedan religion, and were held by those who knew them to be naturally endowed with the characteristics which fitted them for rule. Their theory of justice was good, though their practice was bad; their scheme of taxation was most elaborate and was carried even into a system of death duties which left little for an English Chancellor of the Exchequer to improve. [2]

Lugard himself addressed the Royal Geographical Society in January 1904, where, reading a lengthy paper, he repeated the point often that the Fulani/Hausa language group represented a higher civilization and a society sufficiently structured for the British to work with. His address opened with the following paragraph:

> The Protectorate of Northern Nigeria, concerning which I have been invited to address you this evening, is almost the only part of British tropical Africa which possesses a history

extending over many centuries, or a semi-civilization of its own which dates long prior to the advent of Europeans within its borders. These facts give it a unique interest. [3]

This was in stark contrast to his very poor opinion of the southern and coastal societies, darker in complexion, more decentralized and chaotic in their social organization, politically fractured and individualistic.

This is what he had to say about the Igbo, the largest ethnic group in eastern Nigeria, and arguably the most decentralized of all the tribes of the territory.

> The great Ibo [Igbo] race to the East of the Niger, numbering some 3 million, and their cognate tribes had not developed beyond the stage of primitive savagery. [4]

And so this sort of divergence of opinion along the north/south divide in Nigeria went. It was oft repeated by Lugard and his wife, reinforced by George Goldie and many others, and apparently based on a very superficial understanding of the races.

Nonetheless, what was beyond dispute was the fact that the emirates of the north existed under a comprehensive system of administration that allowed Lugard and his small colonial administration to devolve much of the day-to-day responsibilities of government, tax collection and law to the various emirs, in a system that came to be known as Indirect Rule – or quite simply administration through current structures, seconding the existing leadership while interfering as little as possible with the working machinations of traditional society.

Lugard was able to apply this principle relatively easily in the north of Nigeria, but in the south, particularly in the southeast, the effort was conspicuously less successful. In the absence of strong, centralized leadership, European administrators found it difficult to locate and identify individuals within indigenous society imbued with sufficient authority to act on behalf of the colonial government. The result was often a system of warrant

---

* Flora Shaw, incidentally, was the first to coin the term 'Nigeria'.

chiefs established by the colonial authorities and based on their own interpretations of traditional rule, which very often did not coincide at all with the practicalities of traditional life. Individuals were identified, given the rank of warrant chief, whether they desired it or not, and charged with the responsibility of attending to the colonial government's grass-roots policies on taxation, law and government.

This was similar to many other areas within the colonial spectrum, where local chieftainships were seconded to the colonial government with various grades of authority, and frequently on the government payroll. The effect of this was often to alienate the traditional leadership from the people, causing local chiefs to be identified with the authorities, and in general interfering with and loosening the cohesion of traditional life.

Despite this, Lugard applied many years of his life to the development and proliferation of indirect rule as a soft alternative to the many excesses of government and administration visible in the rule of nations such as the Belgians, Portuguese and French, and also here and there the British. His mantra was best expressed in one of his many academic papers on the subject when he wrote:

> a cardinal principle of British colonial policy [is] that the interests of a large native population shall not be subject to the will ... of a small minority of educated and Europeanized natives.[5]

Members of the Malay Regiment inspect equipment, supplies and documents captured in a raid on a communist terrorist jungle camp. *Source Private Collection*

And nor, for that matter, the interests of a minority population of European settlers and expatriates, or indeed Indians, as the British Colonial Secretary, Sir Victor Cavendish, Lord Devonshire, was at pains to stress in 1923, at a time when Kenyan Indians were beginning to agitate for greater inclusion in the political process in that colony.

Lord Devonshire's comments, made in a speech to the House of Commons, were informed primarily by the League of Nations principle whereby colonizing powers were given mandates over subject territories that had either changed possession or been occupied during the First World War. Notable examples of this in Africa were the mandating of German African territories to Britain, South Africa and France. The new terminology, and indeed the new sentiment, was that of a sacred trust – a sacred trust to nurture the potential to rule of indigenous societies, while at the same time serving notice to large minority settler populations to either reach an acceptable political accommodation with their majority subject groups in a timely manner or risk being overwhelmed. These were Lord Devonshire's words:

> Primarily Kenya is an African territory, and His Majesty's government think it necessary definitely to record their considered opinion that the interests of the African natives must be paramount, and that if, and when, those interests and the interests of the immigrant races should conflict, the former should prevail. Obviously, the interests of the other communities, European, Indian or Arab, must severally

be safeguarded. But in the administration of Kenya His Majesty's government regard themselves as exercising a trust on behalf of the African population, and they are unable to delegate or share this trust, the object of which may be defined as the protection and advancement of the native races.[6]

Serving on the League of Nations Permanent Mandates Commission was none other than Lord Frederick Lugard. The ideals expressed by Lord Devonshire dovetailed very neatly into Lugard's own indirect rule policy, offering him the opportunity to theorize on a merger of white and black rule in what he termed the Dual Mandate. In regard to the future colonial practice of Africa – and here Lugard is referring to territories in Africa administered by the Imperial government that did not contain large and settled white populations – he advocated full indigenous rule under very general imperial oversight, with the view in mind, quite obviously, that indigenous rule would blend better with a collective indigenous psyche, but also, arguably, to prepare Africans for eventual independence.

Lugard died in April 1945 at the age of eighty-seven. As he was taking his final breath, the military formation that he had created, the Royal West African Frontier Force, was contributing, along with many other British and Commonwealth forces, in the drive east and southward into Burma from India, pushing the Japanese out of Southeast Asia, and out of the war. The detonation of the atomic bombs over Japan in August 1945 effectively ended the

RAAF Avro Lincoln bombers at Tengah Air Base, 1950. *Source Private Collection*

British Army patrol crossing a stream during the Mau Mau rebellion. The soldiers carry a variety of weapons, including the L1A1 Self-Loading Rifle, the 9mm Sten Mk5 and the Lee Enfield .303 Rifle No. 5. *Source Private Collection*

war, but ended also a world order. India achieved independence from Britain in 1947, having been promised this in exchange for her participation in the war. From that moment on a domino effect occurred, with British overseas territories claiming and gaining independence one after the other. There was a handful of small wars associated with the process, or emergencies as the British chose to regard them at the time. The main theatres of conflict were Suez, Malaya and Kenya, but the Cyprus Emergency coincided with the same period, and of course there was the ongoing attrition in Northern Ireland.

However, none of the West African territories was divested under conditions of war, or even authentic emergency. The inevitability of independence within a very brief generation became clear immediately after the Second World War, and much British Colonial Service activity in the post-war period was focused on creating the optimum circumstances for a seamless handover of power. Some civil unrest accompanied the process, but this was not directed against an entrenched colonial authority determined not to be moved, or hurried, as was the case in Kenya, and later in Rhodesia, but simply because of the impatience of a newly politicized and enthusiastic population organized and motivated by an educated and ambitious strata of pending national leaders.

The decolonization process in Nigeria, bearing in mind the intricate ethnic tapestry of the region, and the relatively complex systems of government, was quite lengthy, and involved a number of different permutations in the 20 years between the Second Wold War and the dawn of the African liberation period. African independence in general, with very few exceptions, followed a broadly similar pattern. Native education began with the first roots put down by the Christian missionary organizations whose objectives on the whole were to produce local catechists and to promote literacy for the purpose of better disseminating the Christian gospels. By the end of the First World War, a nominally educated strata of the indigenous population was emerging with a somewhat enhanced perception of the modern world. A handful of these were able to gain access to British and American universities, producing in the late 1930s and early 1940s a generation of highly educated and politicized Africans who began to drive the pace and direction of the independence process.

In Nigeria there were many regional and ethnic nuances that both advanced and complicated this process. The amalgamation of the northern and southern protectorates of Nigeria in 1914 was something of a blunder inasmuch as it attempted to forge a single territory out of two radically different, and in many ways mutually antagonistic, social blocs.

Among the hundreds of languages spoken in Nigeria, there are seven that dominate, these are Hausa, Igbo, Yoruba, Ibibio, Edo, Fulfulde, and Kanuri. Among these the three principal languages are Hausa, Yoruba and Igbo, spoken respectively by ethnic groupings of the same name. In very general terms, the Hausa–Fulani group dominated the north of the country, north of the Benue–Niger River confluence and the Yoruba–Igbo group the south. The Yoruba occupy the territories west of the Niger River and the Igbo those to the east bordering Cameroon. The Yoruba and Igbo share the single commonality of not being Muslim, creating the essential and irreconcilable faultline that existed between north and south in Nigeria on the eve of independence.

Such was the general lie of the land, and the British broadly subdivided the region into these individual blocs. The south, by dint of its proximity to the coast, but also because of the relative adaptability of the people, received the early attentions of Christian missionaries who introduced selective literacy and education, primarily, as has been noted, for the purpose of producing local catechists to further disseminate the gospels. The Islamized north obviously resisted any Christian intrusion, and so education in that region remained Koranic, and consequently of little real value in the modern world. As the 20th century dawned, and the protectorates fell under the administration of the British, education was formalized and expanded, but again it was the south that benefitted most. In the north, that very theocracy so esteemed by the British proved to be the instrument of its own social stagnation.

The southern people embraced education as just one of the many potentialities of modern life. The Igbo, from being regarded as pagans and cannibals a few decades earlier, and unworthy of any civilized standards, emerged from the early 1920s onward as the most progressive and adaptable of all the Nigerian ethnic groups. Very quickly, educated Igbos began to dominate the lower strata of the civil service, the blue-collar levels of industry, teaching, nursing, the trades, small business, the junior and senior NCO levels of the police and the army and of course the huge corps of Christian catechists and preachers that the missions produced in ever-increasing numbers. Other groups were represented, of course, but it was the Igbo that tended to dominate.

In the north the complexion was very different. There were insufficient locally educated technocrats and functionaries available to run the systems of government, the postal service, the railways and other key institutions, creating a situation where expatriate pockets of southerners, particularly Igbo, flourished in all the major centres in the north, and in fact in every key centre in the combined territories. Soon local business was dominated by the Igbo, as were the emerging political and social organizations, the proto-nationalism of Nigeria, all of which tended to identify the Igbo as aggressive, entrepreneurial and highly adaptable.

It was in the north that the feeling of cultural exclusivity was most

pronounced and here too that the Igbo had in recent years migrated in large numbers. By the late 1950s they had become established, widely dispersed and extremely influential. The xenophobia peculiar to hardline Islam was very much a factor in the perceived threat against the cultural autonomy of the north. The exclusivity of Islam, the higher social values associated with Islam, and the right to govern implied by Islam, all carried great social gravitas in the north, but in Nigeria as a whole they simply presented the opportunities for highly educated southerners to fill the technical and administrative vacuum left by those too cultured to be learned.

Slavery played no small part in all this. The emirates of the north had been central to the local slave trade, and southern tribesmen had tended to be at the receiving end of this. The abolition of slavery might have stamped out the practice, but the mindset was very much alive. Southern blacks, as educated as they might be, were plebeian, vulgar and dangerous. They were slaves. An inferior race. No amount of social conditioning or statutory equality could change that fundamental state of mind.[*] Southerners might be tolerated under colonial protection, but in general they were vulnerable and exposed.

This might seem overly dramatic in any other context. Recent history has taught the world to take African ethnic discomfiture extremely seriously indeed. Coinciding with Nigerian independence was Congolese independence. The complex ethnic make-up of the ex-Belgian territory, combined with a hurried and ill-prepared departure, plunged the Congo, within a few months of independence, into an imbroglio of ethnic bloodletting that would in many ways come to define African civil war and political disturbance. The Congolese situation was very similar to Nigeria, with the key difference being that the British had minutely prepared their departure, while the Belgians had done no such thing.

In his final published work, *There Was A Country*, Igbo writer Chinua Achebe reflected deeply on his own experience during the Biafran War and commented thus: "Nigerians will probably achieve consensus on no other matter than their common resentment of the Igbo."[7] Why this hatred of one ethnic group was so visceral and so universal is impossible for an outsider to guess. No doubt it has been formed over millennia, and informed by layers of history that are imponderable to any but those engaged in it, and perhaps even to many of them.

To what extent the British understood this dynamic, or even needed to understand it, is a matter of debate, but what is indisputable is that they observed its existence, mapped its basic geographic parameters and worked with them in their design of the Nigerian federation. The emerging Nigerian black nationalists, whose ideological fire was often damped by streamlined access to jobs in the civil services, ran hot and cold on the matter of federation, and they tended to be less ardent in their quest for independence than others in Africa since the British

---

* It is worth clarifying the point that slavery as it had traditionally been practised in northern Nigeria was not on a comparable level to the trans-Atlantic slave trade. Slavery was institutionalized, practised very loosely and was very seldom permanent. The residual race sentiments associated with slavery were, however, acute.

Oliver Lyttelton, 1st Viscount Chandos.

A young Abubakar Tafawa Balewa. *Source ynaija.com*

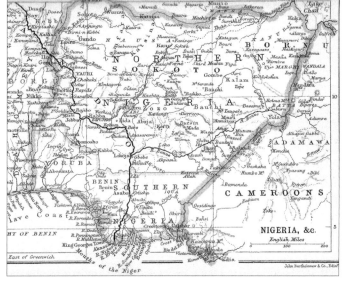

Southern and northern Nigeria c. 1914.
Cartographer John Bartholomew & Co. Edinburgh

of the regions.* These were appointed deputies, not elected, and each functioned under the oversight of a governor general, but an advance had been made, an advance that stressed the unity of Nigeria at a time when the debate was very much about the wisdom of unification in the face of such an obvious ethnic centrifuge.

Thereafter calls for full independence began to gather tempo. The southern regions in general were most vociferous in this demand, while the north was much more reserved. The reason for this, once again, was a fear of what independence might mean in terms of rights and guarantees within an independent nation state. The north owed its predominance to British protections, and naturally northern leaders were quick to recognize the likely ramifications of a British departure.

The problem with the Richards Constitution was that it had been drafted and formalized in closed session with no consultation with local political opinion at all. Unofficial Nigerian representation was by appointment at the discretion of the colonial government or the native administration. All this was very much in keeping with colonial service practice at the time, but the net effect was renewed protest from across the nationalist spectrum until a second iteration began with the drafting of the Macpherson Constitution of 1951.

The main debate in the formulation of this new document, named, once again, after the territorial governor of the moment, was the question of regionalism in a federal context. There were many, in particular in the south, who argued for a unitary state without separate regional identities, while in the north, opinion tended to be that a unitary state would bind the destiny of the north too tightly with that of the south.†

The North would therefore be the main engine of a federal solution in Nigeria, but by the time of the 1950 constitutional conference, held in Ibadan and attended by a spectrum of local nationalist leaders, most major voices in Nigeria had come to recognize that a federal, not a unitary system was, not only inevitable but perhaps even desirable too. The territory had by the end of the 1950s tangibly polarized into three regions, leaving no doubt in anyone's mind that the social, cultural and political differences within Nigeria precluded any hopes for a unitary state.

In the meanwhile the legislative structure of the territory was further modified. The central legislature became a house of representatives, but with significant power devolved to regional legislatures, with, for the first time in Nigerian history, an authentic general election mooted to return the various members. Of course, for the time being, the entire structure would remain under imperial supervision, in the person of Governor General Sir John Stuart Macpherson overseeing a majority European cabinet.

However, independence was now simply a matter of time, and the succeeding constitutional conference was chaired by the British secretary of state for the colonies, Oliver Lyttelton, 1st Viscount Chandos, which gives some indication of how seriously the matter

were by then completely reconciled to their own departure. For Nigeria, it was not a case of if independence would take place, simply what would be its character when it did. The colony had begun as a commercial venture, and notwithstanding certain social experiments conducted by men like Frederick Lugard, it had remained a commercial venture. By the end of the 1950s, contracts had been signed, the right people put in place and a lucrative future for all assured. All that really remained was to prepare the ground.

It was soon after the Second World War that visible signs of change began to appear. A great many more educated blacks began to assume positions at senior levels of the civil service and in the police and army. In 1947 there had been only some 182 Nigerians serving at a senior level in the civil service. This figure is somewhat dependent on the definition of senior, but certainly by independence in 1960 there were several thousand senior Nigerian civil servants by any definition.[8]

Such was also the case on a legislative level. With the introduction of a revised constitution in 1947 an indigenous majority was introduced into the house with specified representation from each

---

* The Richards Constitution of 1947, so named after the governor general of the period.

† The application of Islamic, or *Sha'ria* law in the north was very much at the core of this debate.

was being regarded in Whitehall. The Lyttelton Constitution, formalized in 1954, was to be the independence constitution of Nigeria, and the British government was extremely anxious that the devolution of authority to Nigeria should be as seamless and painless as possible. A great deal of national prestige was pinned on the result, and as a consequence no small amount of political energy was applied to ensuring its success.

In essence, the federal structure of Nigeria was confirmed, with a strengthened federal legislature supported by three regional legislatures, each with enhanced powers, and with the regions retaining an essentially ethnic character. In 1957, Alhaji Sir Abubakar Tafawa Balewa was confirmed as chief minister, effectively prime minister, under the largely ceremonial, but nonetheless extremely observant office of the governor general, Sir James Wilson Robertson, who remained a British official.*

Abubakar Tafawa Balewa was a northerner, a concession to the fact that the north considered itself a senior partner in the federation, which in many practical ways it was, but at the same time he was neither Hausa nor Fulani. His origins, in fact, were relatively humble, but more unusually, he was highly educated, well travelled, uncommonly worldly and generally secular in outlook. He was a tall, angular-featured man, elegant in stature, flamboyant and articulate. He reflected the aristocratic flavour of the north while at the same time being fluent in the language of modern political practice.

As the curtain closed on the 1950s, and with a relatively successful transition of power in Ghana in 1957 under its belt, and even more so thanks to the sheer weight of effort applied to the formula, the British had good reason to feel confident that Nigeria would emerge, on some level, as a vindication of a century or more of moderate, even-handed and nurturing British rule. This, at least, was the hope. The discovery of oil in the Delta region in 1956 liberated Nigeria from dependence on agricultural exports to sustain her economy, and with the best-educated, indigenous workforce in Africa to draw on, the omens were good. Nigeria had the potential to emerge as a wealthy, stable and egalitarian society, if only the constitutional framework put in place by the departing British could contain internal ethnic divisions. It remained to be seen if this could be achieved.

However, it very quickly became clear that it could not. The federal structure defined by the Lyttelton Constitution simply highlighted ethnic separation in Nigeria and did nothing to ameliorate it. The three-part division of the country – north, east and west – conformed closely to the broad ethnic divisions of Hausa–Fulani in the north, Yoruba in the west and Igbo in the east. Differing agendas, deep-rooted social polarities and the peculiarities of power politics in the wider region proved inimitable to the Westminster-style parliamentary system that the British had so fervently hoped would foment a miracle in Africa.

The handover could not be faulted. British expatriates quietly left the country during the closing months of the 1950s, opening up space in the public and private sectors for educated Nigerians to occupy, smoothly implementing a strategy for transition that had been in place long before Nigerian nationalist agitation sought to hurry matters along.

The problem lay in ethnic identity and regionalism. The 1959 general election, however, did at least produce a credible government, ushering in a republic that survived for almost six years. This was enough time for the British to sever all political ties, nullify any latent responsibility and forge lucrative business and economic relationships with the incoming leaders of the country, very often on any terms applicable, which in Nigeria immediately necessitated mind-numbing levels of corruption at almost every level.

As was not altogether unexpected, the Northern People's Congress (NPC), led by the doyen of northern politics, Sir Ahmadu Bello, gained a majority of seats in the federal house of representatives. The east was dominated by the National Council of Nigerian Citizens (NCNC), headed by veteran Igbo–Nigerian nationalist Dr Nnamdi Azikiwe, while the west fell under the temporary control of Chief Obafemi Awolowo.

Almost immediately a series of crises began to gnaw at the credibility of the federation. A split in the ranks of the Action Party in western Nigeria precipitated a state of emergency and a series of deeply questionable political manoeuvres at a regional and federal level. This served notice of the fact that the style and standard of political behaviour in the ex-colony had changed irrevocably. The entire process devolved very quickly into an ethnocentric jostle for power and control at all levels, with the understanding that this would align individuals and groups to gain access to the resources of state on the scale of a virtual feeding frenzy.

This fact was highlighted by a census conducted in 1962 that was intended to supersede a previous census undertaken by the British in 1953–4. The latter had been perceived by the general population as pertaining to taxation, so individuals went to incredible lengths to avoid documentation. Conversely, the 1962 census was widely perceived as being intended to define the levels of political representation appropriate for each region. The result this time was an astronomical and extremely mobile population explosion in all regions that exceeded the reproductive capacity of all women of child-bearing age in the region by several hundred per cent.

In the end two attempts were made, in 1962 and 1963, to gain some sort of accurate representation of the general population, but ultimately the effort was abandoned, a general conclusion was reached and the matter was filed away as yet further evidence of the new order. In the meanwhile the political crisis in the west had degenerated into ongoing and bloody factional turmoil, with the federal government lacking either the appetite or the ability to respond. Corruption on every level, but most blatantly at a federal level, had so compromised the political process that by the end of 1965 it had become generally accepted that only some sort of military intervention could return the federation to order.

And this was indeed what occurred. In January 1966 the first in a succession of military coups and interventions began which set the tone for the next 33 years of military rule in Nigeria. But

---

* Alhaji is an honorific title denoting a pilgrim who has completed the Hajj.

before we move on to trace the role of the military in Nigerian politics, and the events of the civil war, one final word from Chinua Achebe on the matter of Igbo status in Nigerian society would be appropriate.

There Was a Country offers a general but very insightful view of the episode, and in particular the travails of the Igbo people during this period. As in all matters of ethnic tension and rivalry, demonization and canonization tend to characterize the opposing views, but Achebe concludes that the astonishing lead the Igbo people in general managed to gain in matters of education, and in terms of their ability to navigate within modern politics, business and administration, certainly was accompanied by a certain amount of showiness and display, and no small amount of hubris. But he also makes the point that the energy, achievement and competitive individualism of the Igbo was a resource that could, and should have been harnessed by the first generation of leaders

in Nigeria to drive forward the development and modernization of an emerging nation state.

> Nigeria's pathetic attempt to crush these idiosyncrasies rather than celebrate them is one of the fundamental reasons the country has not developed as it should and has emerged as a laughing stock.[9]

It is debatable whether Nigeria was ever a laughing stock, but there can be no doubt that an opportunity was missed during this period. Attitudes to the Igbo people, in particular in the north of the country where they numbered in the hundreds of thousands, possibly even over a million, set in motion a series of responses, purges and pogroms that established a pattern of Nigerian political, military and social development, the residue of which is still very evident today.

CHAPTER ONE:
COUPS AND COUNTER-COUPS

Coups succeed coups. We will never be at peace again.
– Major Hassan Katsina, January 1966

In the early hours of Saturday, 15 January 1966, Nigerian prime minister Tafawa Balewa wrapped up a late-night meeting with three cabinet ministers at his official residence in the Ikoyi neighbourhood of Lagos, and had begun to prepare to retire for the night when he became aware that some sort of a conflagration was taking place at the gates of his walled compound. There, a small contingent of troops under the command of Major Emmanuel Ifeajuna, a brigade major at 2 Brigade HQ in Lagos, and one of five majors central to the planning and execution of the January 1966 coup, was demanding entrance. The police detachment at the gate was overpowered, after which the rebel troops forced members of the domestic staff to lead them into the residence and into the bedroom of the prime minister.

There Tafawa Balewa met the intruders with calm composure, requesting that he be allowed time to pray before his arrest. Then, wearing slippers and a white gown, he was led away from the residence and placed inside a waiting military vehicle in which he was driven away in the darkness, to be neither heard of nor seen alive again.

There has been a great deal of controversy over the fate of Tafawa Balewa in the hours following his abduction. Eyewitnesses at the scene report that he was saluted by troops and assured that he was not to be held personally accountable for the political situation in Nigeria. He was, however, found dead in a plantation not far from the town of Ifo, leaning against a tree in a seated position. He had apparently been en route to Calabar in the far southeast of the country. The assumption has always been that he was murdered,

but circumstantial evidence tends not to support this, while recent reminiscences of surviving players in the episode have suggested that he died of an asthmatic attack during the process of his abduction and removal from Lagos.

Elsewhere in the country a similar series of coordinated actions was in progress. A coup masterminded by five Nigerian army majors was underway. The homestead of the northern premier, the Sarduna of Sokoto, Sir Ahmadu Bello, was surrounded by rebel troops under the command of Major Chukwuma Nzeogwu, who subjected the Sarduna's lodge to a withering assault from a single anti-tank rocket launcher, probably an RPG-7, before the lodge was entered, the Sarduna was located and shot dead immediately by Major Nzeogwu himself.[10]

Similar scenarios played out in the other regions, along with the running to ground and killing of several high-ranking army command elements in a coup that appears in general to have been somewhat haphazardly planned. The decision to take or spare the lives of individual targets, and there were quite a list of these, was left to the discretion of the participating officers who were tasked with particular regional operations. In this regard the killings of Tafawa Balewa and Ahmadu Bello were ill advised to say the least, and what is more, the failure of the coup plotters to locate and liquidate the most vital target under the circumstances, the General Officer Commanding, Major-General Johnson Aguiyi-Ironsi, was an absolute disaster.

Aguiyi-Ironsi in fact appeared to lead a bit of a charmed life for those few vital hours, adroitly keeping one step ahead of mutinous troops once he had become aware of what was afoot. It is worth noting that Aguiyi-Ironsi was an Igbo, as were a majority of the coup plotters, which presented an

Northern Nigerian premier, the
Sarduna of Sokoto, Sir Ahmadu Bello.
Source nairaland.com

Sir Ahmadu Bello in Northern Nigeria.
*Source University of Saskatchewan archives
& special collections*

Ahmadu Bello addresses a political meeting.
Source University of Saskatchewan archives & special collections

reporting on the Nigerian Civil War for the BBC, and he produced his book, *The Biafra Story*, in 1969, before the war had in fact concluded. In it Forsyth enthused on the merits of Aguiyi-Ironsi, whose career he had obviously researched in some detail.

Aguiyi-Ironsi was born in the picturesque eastern town of Umuahia in 1924 where he was partially educated, being further educated somewhat later in Kano, in the north of Nigeria. He enlisted as a private soldier in the 7th Battalion the Nigerian Regiment, the Royal West African Frontier Force, on 2 February 1942. His misfortune at that time was that his service did not take him overseas as it did a great many West African servicemen who enlisted in the RWAFF. He instead remained in Nigeria, concluding the war in 1946 with the post of company sergeant-major. From there his rise through the ranks of the army was rapid. He was among the best and the brightest chosen to attend officer cadet training in Britain as part of a phased indigenization of the armed forces in preparation for independence in 1960.[*] In 1949 he was commissioned second lieutenant to the West African Command Headquarters in Accra, Ghana, and thereafter to the ordnance depot in Lagos before being transferred to an infantry regiment. As a full lieutenant he served as aide-de-camp to governor Sir John Macpherson, also attending the 1953 coronation. In 1955, by then a major, he was appointed equerry to Queen Elizabeth II during her 1956 visit to Nigeria.

This promising trajectory continued, and by 1960 Aguiyi-Ironsi had achieved the rank of lieutenant-colonel, and his first major command, the 5th Battalion based in Kano in the north of Nigeria. That same year he was given command of Nigerian forces serving in the Congo as part of the wider United Nations deployment. He returned to the Congo in 1964 with the temporary rank of major-general in order to command the entire UN force as the first indigenous African solder to achieve that rank. Upon his return to Nigeria, he was reverted to the rank of brigadier, but when appointed first general officer commanding in 1965, upon the expiry of the tenure of the last serving British officer, Major-General Welby-Everard, he did so once again at the rank of major-general.

This was all in all the extraordinary career path of an extremely impressive soldier. As a head of state however, Aguiyi-Ironsi was less impressive. His signature failing during the six months that he was in office was his determination to be fair-minded, honest, ethnically impartial and manifestly transparent, all of which runs so contrary to the Nigerian political mindset that his tenure was doomed almost before it began.

The initial popular response to the coup was overwhelmingly positive. Apart from imprisoning the principal coup plotters,

interesting conundrum for analysts later attempting to portray the coup as an Igbo plot to seize power in the country. In point of fact, and notwithstanding Aguiyi-Ironsi's subsequent stifling, and then crushing of the coup, enough will existed in many quarters of the country to portray the episode thus that it still, in the minds of many observers, remained an all-Igbo affair.

Another point worth noting is that once the dust had settled and the coup had been effectively crushed, the military nonetheless very readily assumed power, installing military commander Aguiyi-Ironsi as head of state, which, even if, as is generally accepted to date in disinterested circles, the coup did not have overtly ethnocentric overtones, it nonetheless resulted in an Igbo head of state.

Major-General Johnston Aguiyi-Ironsi, or Johnny Ironsides as he was affectionately known in wider military circles, was an interesting character who might bear a moment of more detailed examination. One of the most interesting and engaging, although not altogether reliable, accounts of the Nigerian Civil War in general circulation is that written by Frederick Forsyth, a British popular author and occasional political commentator. Forsyth began his writing career as a print and media journalist,

---

[*] Aguiyi-Ironsi was an alumni of Britain's Camberley Staff College and the School of Infantry at Warminster.

Major Chukwuma Nzeogwu.
Source abiyamo.com

Major-General Johnson Aguiyi-Ironsi, aka Johnny Ironsides.

Nigerian troops guard a government building in Lagos during the 1966 coup. *Source Private Collection*

purging the main administrative structures and establishing military governors in each of the three territories of the federation, Aguiyi-Ironsi established a think-tank to identify where and how things had gone so horribly wrong, and to come up with a solution. In fact, the problem seemed quite obvious. It had been the federal system and the entrenched regionalism that had been the foundation of the collapse of the first republic, so a series of commissions was established to look into the matter. A general consensus was reasonably quickly reached, tending to be driven by the south, that a unitary republic would be a desirable alternative to the current federal structure.

Aguiyi-Ironsi accepted this fact, although he also seemed quite cognizant of the dangers of such a move. As usual it was in the north where a merger of the human and political resources of Nigeria as a whole represented the greatest danger, and for all the usual reasons. However, when weighed up as a whole, it appeared, on the surface, that unification would be a popular solution to the current crisis, which led in May 1966 to a constitutional suspension and modification decree, what came to be known as the Unification Decree, and which in essence transformed the regions into a series of provinces with broadly unchanged borders and a largely unaltered system of administration. It is worth noting that under military rule the country was being governed on a unitary basis anyway, with a supreme military council at the centre and a military governor in each region, each following an essentially military chain of command. The Unification Decree really just formalized and codified this fact.

However, from within the fertile seedbed of dispossessed northern politicians and functionaries the first shoots of a renewed anti-Igbo movement began to flower. An Igbo military chief, Igbo coup plotters who had been spared execution and were now imprisoned mainly in the east, an Igbo-dominated commission of inquiry into the terms of unification, and the general jubilation in the east at the delivery of the Unification Decree, all presented the opportunity for a whispering campaign to stir up and utilize all the old and well-established fears and grievances of a lethargic north against the dynamic and ebullient south.

And so it was. The northern leadership besieged the local military governor with threats of secession, a disturbance which reached State House, causing Aguiyi-Ironsi to pour oil on troubled waters by attempting to achieve all things for all people. In the meanwhile the early breezes of a pogrom began to drift through the expatriate cantons of the northern and western cities while a disgruntled northern leadership fanned the embers of xenophobia, always found to be glowing under a very thin layer of nationalistic ash.

When the tempest was unleashed, the sheer organization behind it belied subsequent claims of spontaneity and improvisation. Attacks against expatriate Igbos began on 29 May, a few days after the public announcement of the Unification Decree, beginning in the northern capital of Kaduna, but very quickly spreading as far afield as Kano, Jos, Zaria, Gusau, Sokoto, Katsina, Bauchi and Funtua, to name but a few.* Well-organized gangs began hunting down and targeting easterners in their midst, killing and maiming with clubs, daggers, machetes, bows and arrows, and indeed any other improvised weapons that came to hand.

Insofar as there being any grassroots ideology associated with this bout of fratricidal aggression, it was secession. What sloganeering there was tended to underline this fact, and much

---

* Author: I make use of the term expatriate in this context to underline the extent to which regional identity marked individual Nigerians as they migrated or translocated within the national boundaries of the federation/republic.

Nigerian troops armed with brand-new FN FAL rifles and GPLMG machine guns guard government installations, 1966. *Source Private Collection*

of the pressure that the military government faced from the north was apt to be emphasized by ongoing and increasingly strident calls for secession.

In the context of the Nigerian Civil War, which is the focus of this narrative, this episode has been judged extremely important. Southerners, but Igbos in particular, had been given a preview of the type of institutionalized violence that had in fact been tangible in the wings since the earliest iterations of modern Nigeria. In the first instance the British had been on hand to moderate emotions, and in the second, during the lifespan of the first republic, guarantees of northern ascendency had tended to placate the firebrands, but with the worst-possible scenario looming, and the object of northern hatred very much on hand, northern sentiments exploded into violence in a manner highly suggestive of the fact that this would be neither the worst nor the last popular response of its kind.

Estimates of the death toll are necessarily vague, but no less that 3,000 eastern Nigerians were killed in this purge, which lasted for several weeks over May and June 1966. Very few western Nigerians were targeted, further underlining the orchestrated nature of the episode. It was eastern Nigerians that were specifically identified, with Igbos being the majority. Even Igbos located among mid-western Nigerians were singled out, sending a clear message that the antipathy generally felt for the group was alive and well in greater Nigeria. If discussion in the east regarding secession had a point of genesis, then this would undoubtedly have been it.

However, much worse was to come. The Aguiyi-Ironsi regime response to this episode was placatory, which simply emboldened the northern political elite to make increasingly forceful demands

under the threat of secession. These included the abrogation of the Unification Decree, the trial and severe punishment of the January coup plotters and a guarantee that no investigation into the May–June pogrom would be undertaken. The latter demand, of course, provides as much evidence as could be needed that the emirs of the region were behind the organization of the purges. Along with this, dark rumours began to circulate that an even greater programme of ethnic bloodletting was imminent in the north. News of this reached Aguiyi-Ironsi, who sought the counsel of the chiefs of the army, police and Special Branch who all urged him to discount the rumours as baseless.

About six weeks later, however, on 29 July, army officers from northern Nigeria launched a second coup which toppled the Aguiyi-Ironsi regime, costing Major-General Aguiyi-Ironsi his life, and effectively plunging Nigeria into a crisis from which it would not emerge for another four years. And indeed, Aguiyi-Ironsi was not the only in-house killing. In total seven high-ranking military officers were executed, or murdered, depending on the position from which the killings are viewed. There were very few soldiers at that time who would not have volunteered to serve on any firing squad raised to kill a politician, but the killing of soldiers by soldiers made no sense, and certainly the killing of northern officers enraged the northern rank and file, rendering some sort of revenge action within the wider military structure almost inevitable.

It would, however, be naive to suppose that revenge was the only motivation for the military coup of 6 July 1966. A more subtle cultural anxiety was probably what lay most acutely at the root of what took place. The code word for the commencement of the coup had been *Araba*, meaning, in the Hausa language, secession, which offers the clearest possible indication of what fundamentally drove the coup. The northern sense that the earlier January coup had been an Igbo plot to gain substantive control of the republic had been reinforced by intensive and somewhat subterranean politicking in the north, which buttressed a general perception that swift and prompt action would be required in order to forestall a continuation of the creeping Igbo dominance of Nigeria that had once again become a tangible blip on the energized cultural radar of the north.

The chronology of the July 1966 coup has been exhaustively covered in many forums, and is in its finer detail not specifically relevant to this narrative, other than in the emergence of Aguiyi-Ironsi's ex-military chief of staff, Lieutenant-Colonel Yakubu Gowon, as the new head of the armed forces, and in due course as head of state. Another relevant point, of course, was the systematic killing of men and officers of eastern origin in a manner sadistically brutal, openly blatant and systematic, included among them Aguiyi-Ironsi himself. The military head of state was abducted from the home of the military governor of the west, Lieutenant-Colonel Francis Adekunle Fajuyi, along with a number of others, and subjected to extremely crude abuse and torture before being shot dead.

In the initial massacre of eastern military personnel based in various locations in the north and west (the coup did not affect the east), some 300 individuals were reported killed. However, as the aftermath continued, a more systematic hunt for eastern servicemen in hiding in the north continued. A great many were killed in often horrific circumstances, with only a handful, against almost astronomical odds, succeeding in escaping from the north and across the Niger River into the east. And then in due course, as the killings began to assume genocidal proportions, attention shifted from the military, after which eastern civilians, in particular Igbos, began to be hunted down in cities across the north and west in a miasma of officially orchestrated killings. This ultimately claimed the lives of more than 30,000 individuals, almost all of them Igbo.

Colonel Madiebo recounts the chilling experiences of an army sergeant-major in whose company he spent a night in hiding, alongside other Igbo soldiers, in a hut adjacent to a railway station platform in the small northern town of Ayalagu. This sergeant-major was an Igbo serving in the 3rd Battalion in Kaduna. He survived a massacre in the early hours of 30 July 1966.

> The sergeant-major had very badly bruised hands. He narrated how his commanding officer, Lt-Colonel Okoro was shot at midnight on the 29th, in front of the battalion guard-room. He had been lured out there by his regimental sergeant-major who told him there was a very urgent matter requiring his presence. Having shot the commanding officer, an alarm for a battalion muster parade was sounded, with the battalion yet unaware of the death. On the parade ground, eastern Nigerians were extracted and loaded into waiting trucks. The trucks then drove to Mile 18 on the Ka-duna-Jos road where the passengers were lined up to face firing squads in their turns ... After the execution of each group or truckload, the soldiers inspected the corpses using vehicle head lamps. When they were all certified dead, all valuables on the victims, particularly watches and rings, were removed. The sergeant-major said he was not hit by a bullet but fell down with the dead and lay perfectly still during the inspection. He was covered in [the] blood of others, and only lost his wristwatch during the inspection. Immediately after the inspection and [after] the lights went out, the sergeant-major said he crawled away to safety and later made his way to Jos. The Ibos in Jos gave him a change of clothing and money, and arranged for him to continue his journey to Enugu [the capital of the Eastern Region].

Lieutenant-Colonel Yakubu Gowon. *Source igbofocus.co.uk*

Lieutenant-Colonel Chukwuemeka Odumegwu-Ojukwu.

(Extract from Colonel Alexander A. Madiebo, *The Nigerian Revolution and the Biafran War* (Enugu: Fourth Dimension, 1980). Colonel Madiebo was and Igbo, and commander of the Nigerian Artillery Regiment.)

These events, which took place mainly during the third quarter of 1966, prompted a mass exodus of easterners from the north and west. The feeling among these refugees, as well as the military leadership and the general population of the east, was that the events underway in the rest of Nigeria presaged a systematic extermination of the Igbo, not only in the north and the west, but elsewhere in Nigeria too. The question of eastern secession, an issue that had been fermenting under the surface for some time, now began to be openly mooted as the only practical way that the majority population of the east could hope to survive in Nigeria. The process, however, did not resolve immediately. There followed an inevitable political process, but by the end of 1966, eastern military governor, Lieutenant-Colonel Chukwuemeka Odumegwu-Ojukwu, had privately come to accept that secession was inevitable. Inevitable also would be civil war.

CHAPTER TWO:
THE BIRTH OF BIAFRA AND THE COMMENCEMENT OF THE NIGERIAN CIVIL WAR

Having mandated me to proclaim on your behalf, and in your name, that Eastern Nigeria be a sovereign independent Republic, now, therefore I, Lieutenant-Colonel Chukwuemeka Odumegwu-Ojukwu, Military Governor of Eastern Nigeria, by virtue of the authority, and pursuant to the principles recited above, do hereby solemnly proclaim that the territory and region known as and called Eastern Nigeria together with her continental shelf and territorial waters, shall, henceforth, be an independent sovereign state of the name and title of The Republic of Biafra.

– Lieutenant-Colonel Chukwuemeka
Odumegwu-Ojukwu

One can always look to a novelist to find an accurate portrait of character, and in the case of General Ojukwu, the first and only leader of the Republic of Biafra, there are two to chose from. One was written by Frederick Forsyth and another by Chinua Achebe. Forsyth was a close personal friend of Ojukwu and portrayed him in his book *The Biafra Story* at a time when the war was still very much underway. It is evident that he was in awe of the Biafran leader, representing him as the gifted child of privilege, blessed with rare presence of mind, honesty and an individual desire to achieve. At the time of writing Ojukwu was very much under siege, and one can suppose that Forsyth felt the need to embellish his narrative portraiture with a few heroic elements for the purpose of presenting a better picture of this isolated hero to the international community.

There can be no doubt that General Ojukwu, who was only 34 years old at the onset of the war, was an extraordinary individual. Born in 1933 to the household of an extremely wealthy Igbo business magnate, Sir Louis Odumegu-Ojukwu, 'Emeka' Odumegwu-Ojukwu certainly did enjoy high levels of wealth and privilege in his youth. He was educated at King's College in Lagos, a private academy modelled on the British public school system, founded in 1909, and somewhat more salubrious then than now, which was followed by Epsom College in Surrey, and later Lincoln College, Oxford. Returning to Lagos he rested on his name and credentials for quite a while but eventually, resisting pressure to enter the family business, he joined the civil service, graduating to the army in 1957.

From there his rise was meteoric. Through the medium of British interest in promoting promising local enlisted men, Ojukwu was very quickly returned to the United Kingdom for officer training at Eaton Hall, Chester, emerging as a second lieutenant, followed by further training at Hythe and Warminster. All of this simply added to the polish and lustre of a young man who at that time represented the very cream of West African youth, as well as the hope nurtured by the British that through exposure to the best of the Isles, and certainly to the best of British military tradition, that men like Ojukwu could be the rootstock upon which the fresh buds of Nigerian independence could be permanently grafted.

The January 1966 coup undermined this hope somewhat, but the by-then Colonel Ojukwu was one of few military men who kept a level head, and in the aftermath he was the obvious choice to take over the administrative role of Military Governor of the East. It was from this vantage that he observed the slow implosion of Nigerian unity, watching with dismay as his people were targeted and butchered during the horrific purges of July–August 1966, after which he began to ponder secession as the only possible protection against the very real potential of genocide.

In all of this, Chinua Achebe writes in agreement, but the difference appears to be that Achebe was a professional associate of Ojukwu's in various diplomatic and media roles during the desperate days of the blockade, and was thus more candid in his qualified assessment. In General Ojukwu he saw a man with a colossal ego, and perhaps even more damaging under the circumstances, a snob. Achebe makes the extremely valid point that in a situation such as evolved in Nigeria between 1967 and 1970, the individual personalities of the principal protagonists tend to define the duration of the struggle. In the case of Ojukwu and his antagonist General Yakubu 'Jack' Gowon, Ojukwu looked down on Gowon as being socially inferior, intellectually pedestrian and illegitimate as leader of the Supreme Military Council by dint of the fact the he had not been the senior ranking officer at the time of Aguiyi-Ironsi's death.

Gowon's response to this was as one might expect. History has tended to portray him as a spit-and-polished product of the British military system, and a fine creation of the Royal Military Academy of Sandhurst. But in a mirror reflection of the unshakable sense of self worth instilled in British aristocratic youth, accepting achievement as a matter of birthright, Ojukwu was unable to recognize the accomplishments of a man who probably had better military credentials than he, but who suffered significantly from inferior social flair, limited powers of intellectual reasoning and certainly a general lack of creativity. Gowon's desire to prove himself in the face of this, to not appear weak from his position of strength and to punish his enemy for his insufferable conceit, tended often to overwhelm his tactical assessments of the battlefield.

All this is of vital importance in achieving a clear understanding of the dynamics of the Nigerian Civil War. There were, of course, a great many other nuances that helped paint the character of this, one of the first and most awful African civil conflicts, but personality and ego certainly were among the most potent.

However, in the months subsequent to the July coup, and the pogroms that followed, a political crisis emerged that was much bigger and much more deeply rooted than any of the individual personalities currently dominating the stage. Prior to the coup an estimated 1,300,000 easterners, mainly, but not exclusively, Igbos, had been resident in other regions. Of these about 800,000 were resident in the north and about 500,000 elsewhere in the federation.* Of these, at a conservative estimate, 30,000 did not survive the purge, with an obvious figure far in excess of this of people injured, maimed, displaced and traumatized. It is impossible to overstate the severity of the circumstances and the depth of feeling in the east as a flood of refugees began to make their way across the Niger River with tales of horror that excited all the fear and incredulity to be expected in the home population.

Colonel Ojukwu was therefore not only confronted by a massive refugee problem in a region already land- and resource-pressured, but by the inescapable sense that the combined peoples of the east had no place in the federation, were not wanted as a regional ethnic partner, and that assimilation of the Igbo into the federation was being suffered for no better reason than the oil revenues it contributed to the federal treasury.

Meanwhile, the repatriation of many influential and powerful Igbos back to the east from other regions in the federation bolstered the regional body politic that Ojukwu had at his disposal, giving him a highly productive and influential political circle to work with, but also making it difficult for him to ignore a powerful groundswell of emerging opinion that the only means that the Igbo had to guarantee their survival was to secede from the federation.†

At this time Colonel Gowon, soon to be self promoted to major-general, began to display his own leadership mettle. This mettle, although it did not lack shrewdness of its own, was nonetheless in the early stages very much the shrewdness of others. The most significant other at that time tended to be the incumbent permanent secretaries of departments and ministries who, once civilian heads of departments had been ousted by the military, remained very powerful within the political-administrative establishment in the absence of any meaningful understanding of government on the part of a junta of none-too-clear-thinking soldiers.

The tendency of the establishment then was to try and consolidate the strong core of government embodied in the Supreme Military Council, in the interests, first and foremost, of consolidating power, but of course also in the interests of accruing

wealth which, within the Nigerian system, political supremacy automatically implied. There was, therefore, an inbuilt resistance to the devolution of any power away from the federal core to the regions. This, of course, conflicted sharply with the position of the eastern region, which declared devolution as a basic precondition for the east remaining in the federation. It was clear impasse.

Colonel Gowon, therefore, as something of a man of straw, led a federal political agenda, which was aimed ostensibly at finding a mutually agreeable solution to the eastern secessionist agenda, but at the same time determined to concede absolutely nothing to fairly genuine eastern concerns. The machinations of this agenda consumed the final months of 1966 and the opening months of 1967 in a generally fruitless, largely disingenuous and often overtly threatening process, which Colonel Ojukwu complied with only very superficially, since he also had very little practical interest in compromise.

The process ended with a meeting of all four regional governors, convened in the southern Ghanaian town of Aburi. The objective of the Aburi Conference was to reach some sort of broad agreement on the future complexion of Nigeria. The effort was doomed, however, largely for the reasons cited above, but also because Ojukwu did not recognize Gowon's leadership of the Supreme Military Council, even though the conference fundamentally starred only these two individuals.

Nonetheless, a working formula was achieved that on the surface appeared to favour Ojukwu. Substantial control over the regions would devolve away from the centre, while at the same time the army would be reorganized to redistribute battalions back to their regions of majority representation. This, in theory, would serve to depoliticize the army, although at the same time it was also something of an admission that a complete ethnic merger in Nigeria was, at that point at least, impossible. The net result of this would be that battalions would thereafter tend be loyal first to their ethnicity before any concept of a united federal army. Furthermore it was agreed that the treasury would consider ways to assist eastern refugees and to guarantee payment to date for federal civil servants displaced by the purges. Central responsibility would be reduced to the coordination of common services, inter-regional economic relations, and of course foreign affairs.

All this on paper was extremely encouraging, but in practical terms it was a pipe dream, and it is doubtful whether Ojukwu believed it for a moment. Throughout the process, eastern procurement officers, pre-empting a crisis, had been touring eastern and western Europe acquiring weapons, suggesting, that at the very least, Colonel Ojukwu was spreading his options.

Gowon, on the other hand, had put his signature to the draft document without wielding sufficient authority to carry the powerful permanent secretaries along with him, or even many of the sceptics among his own military colleagues. He has since been portrayed, in the context of the Aburi Conference, as well meaning but witless, naive and ill advised, returning to a federal alignment favoured by his civilian political advisers at the moment he arrived back in Lagos.

---

* Efiks, Ibibios, Anaang, Ejagham, Oron, Ogojas and Ijaws were among the smaller eastern ethnicities singled out for attention during the pogrom.

† These men included the ex-president of the republic, the venerable 'Zik', former governor general Dr Nnamde Azikiwe, former premier Dr Michael Okpara, former civilian governor Dr Francis Ibiam, former judge of the world court Sir Louis Mbanefo, former vice-chancellor of the University of Ibadan Professor Kenneth Dike, and respected academic Professor Eni Njoku.

Frederick Forsyth, who incidentally took very much the above view of Gowon's performance in Aburi, nonetheless acutely described the upshot of the conference with the comment that within "a few days of Gowon's return to Lagos the Aburi agreements began to die on the vine".[11] When the findings of the conference were made public, the communiqué document, unsurprisingly, bore almost no resemblance to what had been agreed at Aburi. Colonel Ojukwu was ready for this and immediately responded by issuing an edict that all federal revenues collected in the east would thereafter be diverted internally to deal with the problem of displaced people, not including oil revenues, which were in any case collected in Lagos. This was fighting talk and, moreover, the mere mention of oil revenues sent shivers down the collective spine of the federation. Gowon responded almost immediately with what was dubbed Decree Eight.

On the surface Decree Eight appeared to be reasonably true to the main points of the Aburi Agreement, but the illusion was broken by the fine print which allowed for all powers devolved by provisions of the Aburi Agreement to be fairly easily retrieved, either through a state of emergency or a simple decision at the centre that such action was necessary. Likewise, a clause was included that regional governors could not exercise their power in a manner detrimental to the centre, the criterion for which would naturally be decided in Lagos.

Decree Eight was promptly rejected in the east, where preparations for separation continued. In Lagos, however, an ebullient Gowon had more to announce. On 23 April 1967, the fact was made public that the three regions of Nigeria would be divided into 12 states, with the east forewarned that stern measures would be taken in the instance of any difficulty generated from there. The political objective of this was to break up the clear ethnic identity of each state and nullify the potential for individual states, such as the east, forming sufficient consensus to secede.

This again ran contrary to the fundamental eastern tenet of greater autonomy in the regions, and as Gowon went ahead with the planning of a reorganized federation, the eastern consultative assembly met and formally empowered Colonel Ojukwu to secede.

Ojukwu accepted the mandate, and in the early hours of 30 May 1967 he read the proclamation of secession against a backdrop of the Biafran flag, addressing a specially invited corps of diplomats, judges and senior public servants at the governor's official residence in Enugu.*

The matter then rested on the federal response. A sense of the calm before the storm descended on the nation, and on the east in particular, as the population held its breath in anticipation. There was a sense that possibly the Supreme Military Council might blink, and the Aburi Agreement be revisited. However, when on 6 July 1967 Nigerian artillery shells began to rain down on the town of Ogoja, ten miles from the border with the north, it was clear that the game was on.

---

* The Biafran flag consisted of horizontal stripes of red, black and green with a rising sun set in the centre.

CHAPTER THREE:
AN UNEQUAL WAR

No one should kid himself that this is a fight between the East and the rest of Nigeria. It is a fight between the North and the Ibo.
– Mallam Kagu, Regional Editor of the *Morning Post*

The Nigerian military high command launched their opening assault on the breakaway region of Biafra in what was initially described as a police action. This, however, was a clear case of the optimism of amateurs. The Nigerian armed forces were configured for peacekeeping and internal security, and the sense of invincibility that infused the rank and file had been honed on no greater challenge than the suppression of unarmed civilians and the killing of disarmed members of its own various battalions. As a consequence of this, the prognostications of a rapid victory over a rag-tag garrison in Biafra tended to excite a great deal of bravado in combination with almost no realistic tactical planning.

The rationale behind the initial attacks launched against the towns of Obudu, Ogoja, Gakem and Nsukka, key strategic points on the north and northeastern border between Biafra and the northern federal region, was to facilitate a quick capture of the eastern regional capital of Enugu, which it was confidently predicted would be achieved in a matter of days, and which would bring the entire matter to a rapid conclusion.

The operation was codenamed Unicord, and was commanded on the ground by Colonel Hassan Katsina, using primarily northern forces drawn from 1 Area Command HQ in Kaduna. These consisted of two brigades comprising three battalions each. 1 Brigade was tasked with the capture of Ogugu and Nsukka, the latter being a university town and an important commercial and administrative centre. From there detached elements would be earmarked to push south and probe the perimeter defence of Enugu, about thirty-five miles farther south. A second column in the form of 2 Brigade was to bear down on Enugu from the east having first captured Ogoja, Obudu and Gakem.

A pattern to the Nigerian advance quickly emerged, one that was followed fairly closely throughout the offensive. At the first sound of heavy guns the local population would melt away into the surrounding bush, remaining incognito for several days as Nigerian troops entered and comprehensively looted each of the

Biafran recruits underwent a short period of training before being sent to the front and had to make do with sticks to practice aiming with. Only the instructor in the foreground has a rifle but he has no magazine so no target practice is possible for his men. *Source Private Collection*

towns, after which the locals would slowly return, welcoming the 'liberators' while variations on 'Keep Nigeria One' posters would begin to appear in various places. Locals would thereafter often join in the looting.

The offensive was premised on a fairly simple plan that relied heavily on communication and coordination, and was based primarily on the expectation of a minimal defence; and indeed the initial Biafran response to this offensive was nothing if not *ad hoc*, with elements that were so poorly assembled and commanded that they proved for the most part to be more of a hindrance to effective military manoeuvre than an asset. Significant numbers of volunteers were armed with nothing better than machetes, viable in close-quarters guerrilla engagements or in the harassment of columns, but hopeless in the face of blanket artillery and mortar fire support as was deployed on both fronts by the Nigerians. In fact, even troops in more orthodox battle order recognized the need for static defences and entrenchments far too late, finding themselves vulnerable to heavy artillery bombardment as Nigerian forces surged toward Gakem, and without artillery or mortars to answer back with, they had no choice but to withdraw.

However, matters were not as desperate as they seemed. Biafran

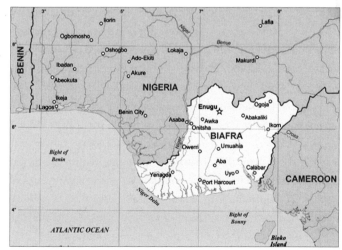

Official Biafran map.

military preparations had been underway for some time, and these early results, although regrettable, did not unduly dismay Colonel Ojukwu, who was fully aware of the strengths and limitations of his force. Initially his strategy was political, and was premised less on any realistic attempt to defeat or turn back the Nigerian federal army than to use this open breach, and the overwhelming

This unit of Nigerian federal troops has just survived a Biafran ambush near the town of Nsukka. *Source Peter Obe*

Colonel Hassan Katsina is quoted to have said: "Personally, I would not feed someone I am fighting against." *The Times*, London, 28 June 1969. *Source abiyamo.com*

Western Premier Chief Awolowo.

conventional assault that followed, in terms of its propaganda potential. His initial hope was that he would be able to swing both local and global public opinion toward the inevitability of the break-up of the federation, and an eventual international recognition of Biafran sovereignty.

Initially there was some hope that the west would either throw its lot in with the east in a war against the north, which would have been a non-war since the current northern-aligned regime would simply have collapsed, and the disintegration of the federation would then have been *de facto*; and for a while there seemed to be some practical optimism that this might occur.

Western Premier Chief Awolowo, although part of the federal political establishment, had yet to formally endorse the federal war effort, leading Ojukwu to anticipate that with a tilt in the right direction, and a credible and spirited military performance against the Nigerian Army, the west might edge toward its own separation. However, as verbiage crept out of the west, supporting the cohesion of the federation, this hope began to diminish.

Thereafter, although accounts vary on which strategy superseded the other, hopes for a total secession began to recede in favour of the east carving a more vital and autonomous role for itself within a new version of the federation, and one supposes for the other regions too. It would seem that there ought to have been a fair hope for this, bearing in mind the past attitudes of the north to federation and unity, but the fact remained that the east had the oil, and in oil lay the bounty.

In this regard Ojukwu was pragmatic in his conception of the battlefield. If the sacrifice of territory was necessary to precipitate these events then so be it, and likewise, if such a sacrifice yielded no tangible political results, which it never did, then the recruitment, training and arming of the Biafran army was underway in preparation for full-scale war.

In fact, international political opinion varied very little throughout the war, with the major international powers remaining generally sympathetic but steadfast in their refusal to recognize the breakaway state, a movement led primarily by Britain under Labour Prime Minister Harold Wilson.

Harold Wilson was somewhat under siege during this period, and had his hands full, both with the diplomatic fallout of the Biafran War and his handling of the Rhodesian crisis and the unilateral declaration of independence (UDI) announced by Rhodesian Prime Minister Ian Smith in 1965. Wilson was something of a left-wing intellectual technocrat, who arguably fumbled both of these issues. However, from the point of view of a humanitarian, which was one part of his complex platform in dealing with the Rhodesian crisis, he and his cabinet showed a remarkable resilience to the spectre of human suffering portrayed by a torrent of newsreels and photo imagery throughout the latter phases of the Nigerian Civil War.

This illustrated to an anguished world the rapid decline of food security in Biafra from austerity to mass starvation, while Britain, to all intents and purposes, maintained a dogged determination

Nigerian troops examine captured Biafran H&K G3 rifles.
Source Private Collection

to back the likely winner of the war, whatever might have been the moral or humanitarian position.* British journalist Michael Leapman, in an article published in *The Independent* in January 1998, and responding to much official documentation on the crisis that only then was being released for public scrutiny, quoted a particular Commonwealth Office briefing document as making the point that: "The sole immediate British interest is to bring the [Nigerian] economy back to a condition in which our substantial trade and investment can be further developed."[12]

As has been noted earlier in this narrative, the British handled the handover of power in Nigeria with consummate skill and attention to detail, offering an almost perfect case study on the planned transition from political and economic predominance in the region to pure economic predominance, doing everything humanly possible to ensure that British commercial interests, in particular within the oil sector, were protected. Obviously then, as now, the bulk of Nigerian foreign earnings were derived from oil, with most major installations located in the east. Shall/BP, then partly owned by the British government, was the largest producer.

After the secession, Ojukwu demanded that royalties for oil production be paid to Biafra and not to the federal government, for obvious reasons. Shell agreed to make a token payment of £250,000, a fairly nominal sum, which the Commonwealth Office tended to support, but which Harold Wilson refused to countenance. This probably had much to do with the fact that Rhodesian UDI had created a not dissimilar situation in southern Africa – a rebel republic pressing Britain for recognition – which, for multiple reasons, Wilson was neither willing nor politically able to permit. And so recognition of Biafra, even if only economic recognition, would have created an extremely dangerous precedent at the time in relation to Rhodesia's expectations or hopes for British recognition. It might be noted that British diplomatic interest in recognizing the internal settlement in Rhodesia in 1979 was derailed by Nigerian economic action that reminded Britain at this crucial moment of the importance of Nigerian oil revenues and foreign currency reserves for the British economy.

United States foreign policy on the matter, first under Lyndon B. Johnson and then Richard Nixon, vacillated in a crisis of moral indecision, but tended in the end to follow the British lead in terms of withholding recognition and support for Biafra. The international response was in general informed very much by the attitudes of the Organization of African Unity, the OAU, and the Commonwealth, but primarily the former. The official position of the OAU tended to be determined by the collective attitude of the majority two-thirds of its members, all of whom maintained that the Nigerian Civil War was an internal affair, and with a general reluctance clearly evident within that forum to tamper with issues of national sovereignty, lest issues of national sovereignty in turn be tampered with, majority recognition of Biafra was withheld. Intervention, or support for any secessionist tendencies, would obviously have sent the wrong message to minority groups in other states in Africa, where the maintenance of colonial-era boundaries was extremely tenuous. And of course there was very little appetite in African corridors of power for too great a scrutiny of Nigeria's human rights record lest others come under scrutiny too. In the event only Ivory Coast, Zambia, Tanzania and Gabon ever formally recognized the breakaway state.[13]

It is also perhaps worth noting that there was a curious alignment in the attitudes of the two global superpowers at that point. The late 1960s saw an upsurge in Soviet and Red Chinese interest and influence in Africa, with a consequent rise in the United States' involvement and concern. This was evident in Soviet and Chinese support for the liberation movements in many emerging hotspots, not least Mozambique and Angola, and certainly the United States and the Soviet Union had chosen very much opposing camps in the Congo crisis. The Soviet Union backed the nationalist followers of Patrice Lumumba while the United States supported the secessionist aspirations of Katangese separatist leader Moise Tshombe. However, in Biafra, both superpowers tended to be supportive of Nigeria, with both withholding support for Biafra, although admittedly, each for quite separate reasons.

United States' support for Nigeria was primarily diplomatic,

* Wilson's handling of the Rhodesian crisis had created a great deal of animosity toward Britain within the Commonwealth and Organization of African Unity, and so Wilson was personally quite circumspect about adding fuel to this diplomatic fire by any action in relation to Biafra that was not in alignment with general African opinion.

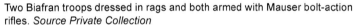

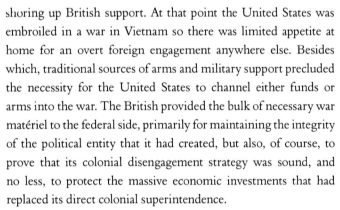

Two Biafran troops dressed in rags and both armed with Mauser bolt-action rifles. *Source Private Collection*

A Nigerian soldier carries his kit 'African style' on top of his US-type steel helmet. *Source John de St Jorre*

shoring up British support. At that point the United States was embroiled in a war in Vietnam so there was limited appetite at home for an overt foreign engagement anywhere else. Besides which, traditional sources of arms and military support precluded the necessity for the United States to channel either funds or arms into the war. The British provided the bulk of necessary war matériel to the federal side, primarily for maintaining the integrity of the political entity that it had created, but also, of course, to prove that its colonial disengagement strategy was sound, and no less, to protect the massive economic investments that had replaced its direct colonial superintendence.

The British, however, were reluctant to conclude any deals on aircraft, fearing an escalation of the war if modern fighter jets and bombers were introduced to the conflict. This offered the Soviet Union the opportunity to tender its assistance. The Eastern Bloc in general had tended to be frozen out of Nigeria in the immediate aftermath of independence, and indeed both subsequent military governments were very cool toward Soviet overtures, but the supply of Soviet aircraft, soon after the onset of the war, broke the ice and gave the Soviet Union access to what had until then been very much a British and United States sphere of influence.[14]

It is also perhaps worth noting that the supply of Soviet aircraft, and the Soviet insistence that only Egyptian pilots be used to fly them, created the circumstances for the only official outside engagement in the war. As will be discussed later, mercenary pilots were engaged to make up for local technical deficiencies, and to some extent Egyptian deficiencies, but the Egyptian personnel were the only foreign combatants seconded directly from the armed forces of another African country.[15]

In the meanwhile, the Nigerian offensive continued with the successful capture by 2 Brigade of the towns of Garkem, Obudu and Ogoja in the east, and the simultaneous advance by 1 Brigade southward, first toward Nsukka, and then Enugu, with the former falling on 26 July and the latter on 4 October 1967.

The Nigerian advance on the whole was cautious and incremental, bearing down on Enugu on two axes that would combine at a point called 9th Mile Corner, near the town of Ngwo, entering the city from the west. The expectation was that Enugu would be heavily fortified and that the defence of the city would be something of a last stand for the Biafrans, upon the understanding common in conventional warfare that the capture of the capital of any territory amounts to an effective check-mate.

In fact the Biafran defence was once again haphazard and opportunistic. The Nigerians advanced in strength with reasonably effective fire support, encountering obstacles and inconveniences en route, but nothing in the way of solid defensive positions or organized resistance. Again the bulk of the Biafran defence consisted of large *ad hoc* levies of machete-wielding tribesmen and a depleted and disorganized garrison. Air defence, a surprisingly bold and effective element of the Biafran armed complement, amounted to one Second World War-vintage Martin B-26 Marauder and a B-25 Mitchell, the former piloted by a Polish, or perhaps Czech national by some accounts, going by the name of 'Kamakazi' Baun, or Brown, and six French-built Alouette III helicopters with mounted door guns from which hand grenades were rained down on advancing Nigerian forces.*

Biafran air operations had mixed results. The Alouettes were deployed with very limited practical effect, although the B-26 penetrated as far west as Lagos, and as far north as Kano, undertaking a number of very credible bombing raids. The raid on Kaduna airfield succeeded in killing and injuring a number of West German instructors who had been training Nigerian pilots to fly Dorniers, resulting in the remainder decamping at 24 hours' notice.†

On the Nigerian side a general lack of advanced intelligence had tended to result in an overestimation of Biafran defence, resulting in a surfeit of caution and a probing advance that may have been successful months earlier.

To the consternation of the Nigerians, this rather amateurish, but nonetheless successful, operation to take Enugu did not result in the fall of Biafra. Instead the city was largely abandoned, and Biafra simply shrunk, but the war continued. The greatest opportunity for an end to the war was in fact a missed opportunity – an extremely narrow escape from the city by Colonel Ojukwu himself. Ojukwu had been asleep in State House when the Nigerians began to enter Enugu. With the first gunfire and mortar barrage he awoke to discover that he had not only been abandoned by his personal aides and guard, but that State House was surround by federal troops. Disguising himself as a servant, the rebel leader calmly stepped out into the grounds of State House and walked away, returning a cheerful wave from a small detachment of federal troops.

Coinciding more or less with the fall of Nsukku, a day earlier on 26 July, the Nigerian 3rd Marine Commando Division launched a surprise and surprisingly well-planned seaborne assault on Bonny Island in the east Niger Delta region. Bonny Island was at that time an extremely important location insofar as it was, and is, the main oil-loading terminal for the Shell/BP pipeline from Port Harcourt.

With the Nigerian victories in the north consolidating in the capture and abandonment of Enugu, and the southern seaboard coming under pressure, Ojukwu revealed a streak of tactical flare at the last minute that might just have turned the tide of the war had the vagaries and complexities of ethnicity and allegiance not intruded. This was the much-storied Operation Torch.

As all of this ducking and feinting had been underway, Ojukwu

---

* Some documentation states three Alouette IIIs.

† The Nigerian Air Force existed in practical terms in name only, until on 13 August 1967 when the Soviet Union commenced delivery of the first of several Egyptian-supplied and -piloted MiG-17s. These were followed by six Il-28 bombers flown by Czech and Egyptian pilots.

had been diligently attending to building a credible Biafran army. In August 1966, the signal for a new paradigm had been sounded when non-eastern troops were redeployed to their region of origin, which left a total of just 240 of the 1st Battalion in situ in Enugu. These were obviously considerably bolstered as fugitive eastern troops from various other federal battalions began to arrive, having escaped the fratricidal killings of July, August and September. Recruitment from among civilian refugees flooding back into the east was also underway, and it almost goes without saying, such was the general feeling among easterners, that the rush to be armed and trained very quickly overwhelmed the capacity of the authorities to supply armaments and training.

Arms supplies were at the onset, and remained throughout the conflict, the single biggest difficulty facing the armed forces of Biafra. Initially Ojukwu was able to secure supply contracts through French, Spanish and Portuguese sources, but as the blockade tightened, and diplomatic difficulties increased, these tended to be limited to regular but inadequate airlifts out of Portugal into one of two viable airstrips within Biafran-controlled territory.

For the time being though, Ojukwu concentrated on establishing an independent military structure. He was himself a military man with a background balanced between logistical and tactical education and experience, and so he was immediately cognizant of the practical requirements of building, training and equipping a credible army. Attention was given in the first instance to the establishment of an officer corps, recruits for which were drawn mainly from the ranks of students and lecturers from the University of Nigeria, which was located in Nsukku. In the meanwhile, a high-level conference of senior army officers was held in Enugu where discussions centred on the best means of formally establishing an eastern command and, of course, on the divisional structure of a new army.

The formation of two new infantry battalions was mooted: 7th and 8th Battalions to be based at Nsukka and Port Harcourt respectively, the former tasked with the defence of the northern frontier and the latter with the Atlantic seaboard. The original 1st Battalion, a remnant of the federal army, remained in reserve in Enugu with the additional task of defending the western borders of Biafra, defined by the Niger River, which by its nature was a fairly formidable defence in and of itself.

To facilitate all this, a training depot was established inside Enugu prison in order to preserve secrecy, although the standards of Nigerian intelligence gathering and analysis rendered it likely that all military preparation underway in Biafra was safely hidden behind a veil of federal ignorance and incompetence.

By the time the first shots were fired in July 1967, the three companies of 7th Battalion had been deployed in the north, with A Company at Okuta, responsible for holding the eight-mile quadrant between Okuta and Onitsha, B Company at Enugu, responsible for the 30-mile defensive line between Okuta and Obolo-Ake, and C Company responsible for defending the lines of communication between the main battalion and a platoon located at Eha Amufu.

South of Port Harcourt, 8th Battalion was broken up into four companies deployed respectively to Ahoada, Calabar, Oron and Bonney. The original 1st Battalion, as mentioned, was retained to secure the capital Enugu, or at least to delay its capture. An additional 4th Battalion was in the process of forming up in the south as hostilities commenced.

Apart from this basic infantry, air force and navy structure – all of which possessed the correct and proper military taxonomies, but were nonetheless extremely *ad hoc* in character and haphazardly trained and armed – Ojukwu added to the mix the Biafran Organization of Freedom Fighters (BOFF), which was part political commissariat, part support battalion, part reconnaissance and part special forces sabotage and counter-insurgency. BOFF, incidentally, was trained by a team of South African instructors led by Colonel Jan Breytenbach, who would, in due course, achieve a great deal of local notoriety and considerable accolades for his work with South African special forces, in particular the founding of 1 Reconnaissance Commando, 32 Battalion and 44 Parachute Battalion.* Breytenbach's observations on the organization and battle readiness of the Biafran armed forces are quite instructive.

> He [Breytenbach] discovered later that despite the splendour of the brigadier's command set-up, the bone china cups, the elegant red tabs, the maps and the magnetic markers, he had no communications whatsoever with his troops. He had no radio, no telex, not even a telephone link.

---

* Colonel Jan Breytenbach is the older brother of writer, painter, poet and staunch South African anti-apartheid activist Breyten Breytenbach.

To keep in touch, he occasionally sent a despatch rider to the front [who] reported the current troop positions, which a staff officer, with a remarkable display of artistic licence and imagination, translated into map markers.[16]

Despite this inauspicious start, the South Africans ultimately were able to forge a convincing guerrilla force out of this top-heavy command system and appallingly inefficient supply network, to the extent that the unit was reasonably quickly operational and achieved credible successes for the period that it was active. It is probably worth pointing out that South Africa was the only friendly power to provide training and support within Biafran borders. Rhodesia and France also provided training, but this was undertaken outside Biafra.

Despite this, BOFF remained the most informal branch of a generally highly informal military structure, commanded by the ex-president of the Nigerian broadcasting service staff union, Colonel Ejike Obumneme. The general officer commanding the Biafran Army was Lieutenant-Colonel Hilary Njoku.

Such was the defence picture on the ground as Nigerian federal forces opened up a firestorm and surged into Biafra, aiming for the head of the snake, Enugu. Ojukwu realized immediately that without some sort of creative and bold action the inevitable capture of Enugu would precipitate a general rout and a rapid collapse of the republic. The result was a brilliant tactical coup, sadly leavened by a disastrous choice of commander. With the pressure building in the north, Ojukwu sought to create a diversion by opening a second front in the west.

CHAPTER FOUR:
OPERATION TORCH

Operation Torch was conceived by the Biafran high command as a means to exploit the fact that the federal Supreme Military Council had rather unwisely respected the wishes of the mid-west region to remain neutral in the conflict. Federal military planners had therefore concentrated operations in the north and south of Biafra, leaving the mid-west as an undefended buffer zone. This was an extraordinary lapse in tactical judgement, because just a brief look at a map of Nigeria will reveal that, with all the main elements of Nigerian force focused in the north, the road from Onitsha, the main river port on the Niger, situated on the east bank in Biafran territory, to Lagos, some 400 miles of virtually undefended territory, was wide open. This left the soft underbelly of the regime dangerously exposed, and could only really have been overlooked on the understanding that the Biafrans lacked any kind of offensive capability. The federal armed forces were concentrated in the north, and east of the Niger River, and were powerless to intervene should any offensive action be attempted, a fact that Colonel Ojukwu was very quick to recognize.

The objectives of Operation Torch were potentially multifaceted. In the first instance it was intended to aim a brigade-strength force toward the administrative centre of the regime, maintaining the flexibility thereafter to plunge a dagger into the heart of the military junta if circumstances permitted, but also if possible to precipitate a general move toward secession in Nigeria by presenting the mid-west with the opportunity of siding with Biafra, and failing this, then at the very least to create a military diversion to ease mounting pressure on the Biafran centre from both the north and the south.

The enigma in the planning of Operation Torch was Ojukwu's choice of commander, made even more imponderable by the fact that the Biafran Army commander, Lieutenant-Colonel Hilary Njoku was kept entirely in the dark regarding the operation until the plan was underway.

Commanding the operation would be Colonel Victor Banjo, an ethnic Yoruba who had been a major in the Nigerian Army, and implicated in the January 1966 coup, possibly unjustly, and

Exhausted Biafran troops rest in a rear position on the Onitsha Front surrounded by boxes of precious ammunition. One soldier is armed with a Czechoslovakian VZ-58 assault rifle which was one of the few modern types in Biafran service. *Source Private Collection*

later imprisoned in Enugu on a charge of attempting to assassinate Major-General Johnson Aguiyi-Ironsi, possibly also unjustly. At the outbreak of war he was released and offered a commission in the Biafran Army, which he accepted. He and Ojukwu had previously been friends, but aside from the propaganda and PR value of a Yoruba officer in his inner circle, it was a quixotic decision at best for Ojukwu to permit Banjo into his inner advisory committee, and certainly a risky decision to place him in command of such a potentially delicate operation as Operation Torch; and even more risky to do so over the head of the army commander.*

On 9 August a mobile brigade of Biafran troops crossed the expanse of the Niger River bridge from Ontisha, and plunged headlong into the mid-west. This was the commencement of Operation Torch. It is interesting to note that there were two respected foreign war correspondents more or less *in situ* at that time, John de St Jorre, reporting for *The Observer* and Frederick Forsyth reporting for the BBC. Both produced books on the conflict that offered completely divergent views on what Operation Torch actually represented.

Forsyth portrays a brigade-strength mobile incursion involving some 3,000 men in a lightning operation that displayed both the military prowess of the men on the ground and the bold planning of those behind the scenes. The impression is left of a hard-fighting column battling its way eastward toward the final goal of Lagos. What follows is a brief excerpt:

> On 20 August the Biafrans stormed into Ore, a town on a crossroads thirty-five miles into the West, 130 miles from Lagos and 230 miles from Enugu. This time the Tivs facing them took a worse beating and disconsolately pulled back in disorder. To observers at the time it appeared that barely ten weeks after the Arab-Israeli War another military phenomenon was about to be witnessed ...[17]

Forsyth, as a close friend of Ojukwu's, is guilty throughout his narrative of an extremely unequal portrayal of the relative performances of the Biafrans and the Nigerians, representing the former universally as heroes and the latter as villains which, in the process of warfare in general is seldom justified, and in African warfare almost never. John de St Jorre, on the other hand, paints an ostensibly more accurate and believable picture of an *ad hoc* militia comprising some 1,000 poorly armed and sparsely trained troops entering an almost completely undefended territory. His most oft-quoted description of the event runs as follows:

---

* Not all accounts concur that Lieutenant-Colonel Hilary Njoku was kept in the dark in regard to the planning of Operation Torch.

The Biafrans 'stormed' through the mid-west not in the usual massive impedimenta of modern warfare but in a bizarre collection of private cars, 'mammy' wagons, cattle and vegetable trucks. The command vehicle was a Peugeot 404 estate car. The whole operation was not carried out by an 'army' or even a brigade (as the Biafrans claimed) but by at most 1,000 men, the majority poorly trained and armed, and many wearing civilian clothes because they had not been issued with uniforms.[18]

Wherever lies the absolute truth, what both men agree upon is this: the federal Supreme Military Council was cruelly rattled by the action and Lagos was thrown into panic. The city had been bombed from the air as the invasion commenced, and with nothing of substance standing between him and the steadily advancing Biafrans, Gowon, again according to some but not all accounts, was poised with a private jet on warmed engines to flee the capital at a moment's notice.

The planning of the operation was surprisingly precise. The assault was intended to proceed on three main axes, north, south and west. The northern force would be deployed toward Auchi to protect the right flank of the invasion, and forestall any attempt by the main Nigerian force still concentrated in and around Nsukka, but poised on two fronts to attack Enugu. The likelihood of the Nigerians having the wherewithal to deploy rapidly and at short notice across the wide expanse of the Niger River and into the mid-west to involve itself in the action was so remote in the short term as to render any defence in that sector rather pointless. More crucially, a southern force would be deployed south to the coastal towns Warri, Sapele and the oil centre of Ughelli to likewise block any Nigerian amphibious landing into the region, but also to seize control of what remained of the Nigerian oil industry. The main force, meanwhile, would advance to Benin City and then Ibadan, and ultimately Lagos. The initial push was conspicuously successful with the southern and central objectives achieved. Within ten hours of crossing Niger River bridge at Onitsha, the mid-west had ostensibly fallen into Biafran hands. The three southern centres of Warri, Sapele, and most importantly Ughelli, were taken, with the northern flank covered by the seizure of the towns of Uromic and Ubiaja. Benin City, the capital of the mid-west, fell without a shot being fired.

Tactically, this spectacular result was achieved as a consequence of there being no organized defence of the mid-west, and not thanks to any particular prowess on the part of the Biafran invasion force. However, this notwithstanding, the doorway to Lagos now lay wide open, and the obvious course of action would have been to maintain the momentum and drive toward the capital as quickly as possible. Supply lines were attenuated and logistics a little chaotic, but the seizure of the capital could have been easily achieved at that moment had Colonel Banjo not opted to remain in Benin City for a week to reorganize and consolidate.

This, of course, is an armchair assessment long after the fact. Some of the unique difficulties Colonel Banjo encountered had

to do with the politics of the situation, which did indeed affect the military circumstances. In the first instance Ojukwu sought to pull the mid-west into the eastern orbit and in a way include it in a greater Biafra, or at the very least into a strategic alliance with Biafra. Forsyth notes rather triumphantly in his book, *The Biafra Story*, that the Biafrans had so far lost a little over 500 square miles of their own territory to the federal advance from the north, but had in the meanwhile seized some 20,000 square miles of federal territory right from under the noses of the Nigerian Army.

On the surface this was so, but without some sort of a conclusive result, such as toppling the government and altering the leadership dynamic in Lagos, there never was much chance that this *coup de main* would ever be permanent.

In the meanwhile, there was indeed a certain amount of kinship and ethnic overlap between the east and the mid-west at that point, and Ojukwu sought to capitalize on this by declaring the invasion as being primarily to prevent the federal government from "forcing the mid-west to enlist to fight against their own people".[19] This aspect of the invasion – the political complicity between east and mid-west in the invasion of August 1967 – is a very grey area in the general written history of the war, and without clear reference from either party, suggestions that Ojukwu and the military governor of the mid-west, Lieutenant-Colonel David Ejoor, met prior to the invasion being launched in order to discuss its implications are not completely implausible. The serpentine nature of Nigerian politics tends to permit speculation on any intrigue, no matter how improbable or expedient, although the events that followed do tend to preclude any suggestion that Ojukwu and Ejoor were in alliance, although it is possible that they were. It is also possible that Colonel Victor Banjo, finding himself in a position to personally influence events, and no doubt to secure some political advantage on his own behalf, acted independently and in defiance of orders from Ojukwu.

On 14 August, five days after the invasion, Colonel Victor Banjo delivered a scheduled radio address to the people of the mid-west to ostensibly explain the objectives of the invasion. In the event, however, the address devolved into a rambling personal testimonial intertwined with a lengthy lament over the threats posed to the federation, concluding with an assurance aimed at the population of the region that the invasion was not a conquest, but a deliverance.

Following closely thereafter was the promulgation of a Biafran decree establishing what would be known as the Republic of Benin under the control of a new military administrator in the form of Major Albert Nwazu Okonkwo. Colonel David Ejoor was relieved of his duties. What followed was a brief and somewhat disorganized quasi-regime characterized by the draconian imposition of curfews and martial law, enforced by an increasingly disaffected and locally unpopular Biafran Army.

The whole business had a chaotic and unstructured feeling, which also caused a general hiatus during which even deeper suggestions of duplicity and subterranean political manoeuvring began to circulate. Ojukwu, monitoring all this in Enugu, was

A Biafran soldier armed with a Lee Enfield rifle stops a civilian car at one of the many roadblocks which hampered travel though war-torn Biafra.
Source Peter Obe

This crudely made Biafran cap badge was worn on the front of the 'Castro'-type field hat.
Source Private Collection

angered and deeply disturbed by the contents of Colonel Banjo's radio address, but despite the urging of his inner circle of advisers, maintained outward confidence in Banjo's command, accepting a litany of reasons for the stalled advance while continuing to urge his commander to maintain the momentum of the invasion beyond its farthest point west of Ore, and on to Lagos.

This, again, is a grey area in the history of the episode. Colonel Banjo became the subject of speculation in Biafra that he had turned traitor, and had conceived a typically complex and twisted plot to first overthrow Ojukwu and bring the rebellion to a close before returning to Nigeria as a hero where he and Chief Awolowo, erstwhile premier of the western region, would topple the government and install himself as military leader and Awolowo as premier. This was according to a confession later extracted from Banjo when he was taken into custody in Biafra, and one can only assume that the means by which the confession was extracted would render it suspect. One of the main reasons why this might be so is that Banjo returned to Biafra having abandoned the invasion and ordered a general retreat.

However, to deal with the sequence of events in their correct order, by mid-September, with the Biafran invasion force effectively stalled at Ore by the political prevarications underway, and with the Nigerians beginning to regroup with the understanding that what it was dealing with now was a war and no longer a police action, the opportunity to seize the initiative and take Lagos had effectively passed. Following a rapid recruitment drive and a week of crash training, the federal 2nd Infantry Division was formed under the command of Colonel Murtala Mohammed and put into action in the mid-west against the stalled Biafrans.*

Ojukwu was said to be beside himself with frustration regarding Banjo's unwillingness or inability to act, and was fast reaching the same conclusion as his key advisers and commanders that Banjo had indeed switched sides. This seemed to be confirmed on 12 September by a sudden and unilateral decision by Banjo to order a withdrawal from Benin City, which Colonel Mohammed did not actually enter in force until over a week later. This was followed

---

* Murtala Mohammed served as Nigerian military leader after the overthrow of Gowon in a coup in 1975.

up by orders to withdraw from Warri, Sapele, Auchi, Igueben and other key positions without a fight, all of which resulted in a total collapse of morale on the part of the Biafran front line troops, theatre-wide, which without doubt influenced the speed and effectiveness of the Nigerian advance on Enugu, and the almost supine defence of that city which allowed the Nigerians to effectively walk in.

Colonel Banjo was summoned to Enugu for an audience with Ojukwu scheduled for 19 September where he would be required to account for his actions. By then it had become generally accepted that Banjo was plotting the assassination of Ojukwu, rightly or wrongly, and so provision was made to arrest him on his arrival at State House, which is precisely what took place. Banjo arrived with and escort of armed supporters, who were diverted by a shrewd police ADC and several bottles of gin, after which Banjo was taken into custody. After the extraction of his confession and a brisk trial by special tribunal, alongside others implicated, Colonel Banjo and his cohorts were shot at dawn on 22 September.

The effect of this whole episode was catastrophic. A shudder of revulsion was felt throughout the Biafran armed forces, along with a consequent, if temporary, collapse in confidence in the military leadership. By the end of September, the triumphant Biafran invasion force was contained within a defensive perimeter in the town of Asaba on the west bank of the Niger River, from where a controlled crossing of the Niger River bridge was undertaken before sections of the bridge were dropped. By 6 October, they were home, two days after the Nigerians had walked into the almost undefended capital of Enugu.

As something of a postscript to this chapter, during the period since the events of August/September 1967 there has been a great deal of military analysis and a large number of books written discussing the affair, with significant associated research undertaken, and the conclusion of more than one observer, among them Olusegun Obasanjo, ex-military leader with the rank of lieutenant-general, and final commander of the 3rd Marine Commando Division during the Nigerian Civil War, is that Colonel Banjo, far from turning traitor, made a tactical decision based on the intelligence available to him that suggested any further advance under the circumstances, bearing in mind the differing military capacities and resources of the two sides, would be suicide.

Once again, in the opaque nature of Nigerian politics, particularly during this period, an absolute judgement on the matter is impossible. Colonel Victor Banjo was tried as a traitor, was convicted as such and died accordingly, and there matters remain.

The Nigerians, however, surging up the Benin–Asaba highway in pursuit of the Biafrans, would very soon commit their own catastrophic military blunder, proving that, even if no treachery was involved, calamitous military incompetence itself weighed extremely heavily on both sides in the conflict.

CHAPTER FIVE:
CROSSING THE NIGER RIVER

Colonel Murtala Mohammed, at the head of a relatively inexperienced division, nonetheless achieved spectacular success in his drive to rid the mid-west of the Biafrans. The Biafrans inevitably found themselves with their backs to the Niger River, facing an oncoming enemy and attempting to execute an ordered crossing of the river over the still intact Niger bridge. Asaba, a large town on the west side of the mile-wide Niger River, was taken by the Nigerians only after a bitter and bloody defence. The battered Biafrans fought a rearguard action as they retreated across the bridge, rigging the entire span with explosives to detonate if the Nigerians made any attempt to cross.

Colonel Mohammed arrived on the banks of the Niger River, forced, with a proverbial mouth full of feathers, to watch as the enemy retreated to the relative safety of Onitsha, located some one and a half miles east on the Biafran side. Mohammed ordered elements of 8 Brigade to effect a river crossing immediately to sustain the momentum of what promised to be a dramatic and comprehensive rout. The immediate reaction of the troops under his command, his junior officers and army HQ was stunned disbelief. As the minutes ticked by, the Biafrans were furiously digging in and preparing defensive positions. A jump operation like that would be suicidal.

Orders were issued from army HQ for 2 Division to stand down from active operations, regroup and reorganize. A more systematic plan to cross the Niger would be required, along with the deployment of specialist equipment and personnel. Mohammed disagreed. His sense was that an immediate follow-up would catch the Biafrans on the back foot and throw open the gate to the defensive core of the Biafran enclave, now seriously threatened from the north and the south.

The effectiveness of command and control between Lagos and the front line was always

Colonel Murtala Mohammed.
Source nairaland.com

A Nigerian officer gives his men instructions before an attack against Biafran defences. *Source Private Collection*

A Nigerian veteran of the Second World War prays before going into action. *Source Private Collection*

questionable. The regionalization of the Nigerian armed forces, and the ethnic suspicion that accompanied this, naturally introduced a degree of autonomy on the part of field commanders over the conduct of any particular campaign, and Colonel Mutala Mohammed was at that moment disinterested in entertaining the advice of army HQ, in particular with the smell of the enemy in his nostrils. He ordered 2 Infantry Division to make the crossing.

The logistics of such an operation would be suicidal even by the most ill-informed observation. The river was at that point a mile wide on average, with a large central series of sandy islands beginning just north of the bridge. The Onitsha side lay on higher ground, with a large port and prison complex on the northern side of the bridge – the side where all the preparations indicated where the Nigerians had chosen to cross. Standards of secrecy were atrocious and no attempt was made to mount a deception, so all Biafran defences were focused on the obvious point of landing, and the adjacent approaches to Onitsha.

The first attempt by 2 Division to cross the Niger was mounted on 12 October 1967 and was achieved fairly easily. Biafran forces did not respond to the flotilla of ferries and assault craft moving slowly across the expanse of the river, even allowing

them to secure a foothold and begin probing patrols into the city of Onitsha. However, as Nigerian troops succumbed to looting and general indiscipline, the Biafrans attacked from well-located entrenched positions, slaughtering the enemy until he was able to regroup with his back to the river and effect a chaotic retreat. There was significant loss of life.

Despite this, and despite plunging morale in 2 Infantry Division, Colonel Mohammed ordered a second crossing just eight days later. Once again, without any attempt to conceal or even change the location of the crossing, forward units were sent across the Niger in a collection of ferry boats and military-grade, waterborne assault craft, clearly visible from the Biafran side where carefully prepositioned troops waited until the hapless flotilla had entered the kill zone before opening fire. Two hours of concentrated fire followed, wreaking havoc among the waterborne troops, sinking all but four of the attacking craft and killing hundreds of Nigerian troops, many of whom drowned.

Against heartfelt resistance from within the division, Colonel Mohammed ordered a third assault configured along almost identical lines. Despite a near mutiny, troops boarded their landing craft and slowly repeated the suicidal operation, reaching

Nigerian soldiers armed with FN FAL rifles defend their position near Ore. *Source Peter Obe*

A Nigerian soldier stands near a sign for the town of Ore which his unit has just entered, having defeated the Biafran defenders.
Source Peter Obe

to within a few hundred yards of the Biafran side before a searing enfilade of fire bore in on them, reducing the flotilla once again to tatters and costing hundreds of lives.

Only then did Colonel Mohammed appear to compute the obvious: the operation was doomed. He then turned his mind to another obvious fact that might more profitably have dawned

on him several weeks earlier – that a crossing of the Niger River farther north, within Nigerian territory, obviating the need for a fighting advance across the river, would be a preferable option to losing whole companies of men in a fruitless effort to cross the river in the face of enemy fire.

Colonel Mohammed's conduct of the operations to cross the Niger River has about it all the elements of gross military misconduct, and yet no word of censure or criticism has ever been officially uttered, and in fact Mohammed's military career continued to flourish after the war, ending with his ascension to the rank of general and the military leadership of the Nigerian state after a coup led against General Gowon in 1975. Mohammed was himself assassinated in an abortive coup a year later, in 1976.

In the meanwhile, the crossing was made at Idah on the Niger River, 68 miles north of Onitsha and safely within federal territory, after which a long, southward, fighting advance began that proved not only to be as costly in human lives and ordnance as had been the three attempts to cross the river at Asaba, but which was fortified and reinforced to such an extent that no amount of Nigerian military incompetence succeeded in halting it.

From Idah, 2 Infantry Division proceeded eastward, turning south at Nsukku in a substantial convoy comprising multiple troop carriers, armoured personnel carriers, armoured cars and fuel tankers, along with an estimated 14,000 men. Forty miles south of Nsukku, the town of Udi was taken relatively easily, but from there the division ran into the Biafrans and, according to Forsyth, one of the most significant running battles of the war began.[20]

Colonel Mohammed, again displaying an astonishing lack of tactical originality, punched forward with his forces massed into solid phalanxes, sustaining astronomical losses from harassing attacks against the flanks and rear of the formation. However,

Nigerian troops at Obe, armed with an MG42 machine gun and FN FAL semi-automatic rifles. *Source Private Collection*

the sheer weight of the 2 Infantry Division drove forward and eventually succeeded in reaching Akwa, just 35 miles east of Onitsha.

The operational losses sustained by the division had been extremely heavy, but the Biafrans, already poorly armed and supplied, and significantly depleted from the onset, were utterly exhausted and would have been able to do little if Mohammed had opted to press forward immediately, but his decision to pause for 48 hours in order to regroup and reorganize offered Ojukwu the opportunity to pull troops away from a storming advance farther north that had succeeded in recapturing Nsukku, and was threatening Enugu, and concentrate his forces against the 2 Infantry Division advance.

With the addition of two Biafran battalions the fighting thereafter was bitter and bloody, but in recognition of the fact that the advance was unstoppable, the charismatic, if somewhat unstable, Biafran commander Colonel Joe 'Hannibal' Achuzia opted for the shrewd strategy of forming up behind the Nigerians and following them into Onitsha, which was reached on 25 March 1968, in the hope of immediately forcing them out the other side before they could dig in and fortify.* This strategy was deferred by a sustained friendly-fire encounter with another Biafran battalion that delayed the chase for 18 hours, after which the opportunity was effectively lost.

At this point there is a significant diversion of specifics in the

---

* There is no basis why Achuzia enjoyed the nickname Hannibal, but it is likely derived from his daring military adventurism and the success that he enjoyed from extremely creative and unorthodox tactics.

many accounts of what happened next. What is clear is that Achuzia opted not to attempt any kind of direct assault on Onitsha in order to clear the Nigerians out. His force had neither the resources nor the stamina to attempt anything along these lines. Achuzia did, however, according to the most authoritative sources, suspect that a much larger federal force was following behind and would appear in the theatre soon, and thus he advocated very strongly within the informal command forum to return to Abagana, 20 miles or so to the rear, in order to mount an ambush.

This proved to be an inspired tactic, and on 31 March a 106-vehicle convoy carrying 6,000 men and comprising the usual complement of armoured cars, troop carriers and fuel tankers rolled into an expertly laid ambush – and what followed was arguably the most spectacular Biafran coup of the war. The hapless Nigerian force suffered what the depleted Biafrans could throw at them, but it was a chance mortar bomb igniting a fuel tanker and the subsequent 400-metre tongue of flame that incinerated trucks and men in an instant, that generated the most panic. Nigerian soldiers fled in all directions, and into the waiting arms of Biafran infantry. The episode was little less than a massacre.

The confusion generated in the details of many historical accounts concern mainly Colonel Murtala Mohammed's own role in the disaster. It has been cited in several versions that he was a survivor, which would imply that he was part of the convoy, which of course would not have been likely had he been at the head of the force entering Onitsha six days earlier.

Nonetheless, the Abagana ambush provided a much-needed boost to Biafran morale, but in real terms it did very little to alter the gradual reduction of Biafra into a diminishing enclave. According to Forsyth, Colonel Mohammed had entered Biafra with 20,000 men, out of which 2,000 finally reached Onitsha.

Mohammed then crossed the Niger River in the other direction and made his way to Lagos in order to report the results of this rather tarnished victory, after which he was relieved of his operational command, never commandeding a division again. The exhausted and depleted 2 Infantry Division was rotated out and replaced. The Onitsha garrison comprised 5,000 or more divisional troops, who, despite a number of spirited Biafran efforts, could not be dislodged.

CHAPTER SIX:
SOUTHERN OPERATIONS

Tactics is the art of using troops in battle;
strategy is the art of using battles to win the war.
– Carl von Clausewitz

The seizure of Bonny Island was one of the less conspicuously amateur operations of the war, and part of a greater strategy to isolate and starve out the Biafrans whose determination to resist had transformed a police action into a conventional war. The southern seaboard was already effectively under a naval blockade, but this within itself was not sufficient to ensure the quarantine of the rebel state from the outside world, so the physical domination of the southern coast became necessary. This, of course, would also complete the strangulating encirclement of Biafra, which in military terms would facilitate the creeping gain of territory, compressing the rebellion into an ever-diminishing core that would eventually, and inevitably, cause its collapse.

The region of the Niger Delta is a geographically perplexing maze of inlets, mangrove swamps and tropical verdure that stretches over thousands of square miles, and which historically so confused early maritime cartographers that its function as the outlet of the mighty Niger River to the sea remained an unknown geographic fact until deep into the 19th century. The potential within the entire region for a cat-and-mouse game of blockade evasion was so great that the difficult military decision to occupy it was made as soon as the realization was reached that the federation had a war on its hands.*

Bonny Island was an obvious choice as a point of first landfall on the coast of Biafra, thanks to its commanding position on the coast, but also because of its importance as a petroleum-handling facility, which quite obviously would amplify the general effect of economic sanctions against the mainland. From Bonny, in theory, further military operations to take, or at least compromise, the other main regional centres of Calabar and Oron, also important oil centres, would be relatively easy.

The assault on Bonny Island was one of the better-conceived and more professionally executed operations of the war. Porous intelligence had to a great extent invited earlier catastrophes, so the planning of the operation to take Bonny remained top secret, augmented with the circulation of a rather fanciful deception that the Nigerians intended to land in the riverine regions of the mid-west as an overall plan to gain absolute control of this sector of Nigerian oil production. The mid-west, after all, had declared itself neutral at the onset of hostilities, and so it is arguable whether this feint really fooled anyone.

The Biafrans were nonetheless taken by surprise, simply because the perceived complexity of seaborne operations against the Biafran coast tended to preclude, in the minds of military planners, the possibility of federal forces attempting anything along those lines. It is also worth noting that, like the Nigerians, Biafran intelligence was never really exceptional, and nor in many respects was its

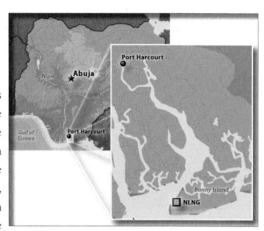

Top: A schematic representation of the geographical position of Bonny Island.

Above: Biafran commander Colonel Joe 'Hannibal' Achuzia.

---

* This realization came with the invasion of the mid-west and the debacle of the Niger crossing. It had become clear then that the Biafrans intended to fight it out, ostensibly to the last man.

Both the Nigerian Army and the armed forces of the secessionist Biafrans made extensive use of Land Rovers. The example shown here was used by the mercenary Rolf Steiner, who commanded the 4th Commando Brigade (later the 4th Commando Division) for much of the war. It was painted like most Biafran vehicles: green overall, with 'leopard spots' in light brown and black. (Artwork by David Bocquelet)

Nigeria acquired a total of 40 Daimler FV701 Ferret Mk.2 and 136 Panhard AML-60 and AML-90 armoured cars during the 1960s. The Ferret was armed with a 7.62mm M1919 Browning machinegun installed in a small turret, and had relatively light armour. The AML-90 was armed with a 90mm GIAT F1 low-pressue gun (with 20 rounds) installed in a prominent bustle at the front of the H-90 turret: although weighting just 5.5 tonnes, the AML-90 proved highly reliable, fast and to have an excellent reconnaissance capability. Like the majority of the Nigerian Army's vehicles all Ferrets and AML-90s were left in green overall and appear to have worn no further markings on their sides: some did receive the tactical unit insignia on the right front fender, as shown for the Ferret, but details of these remain unknown. (Artworks by David Bocquelet)

The Alvis FV601 Saladin was a six-wheeled armoured car originally developed by Crossly Motors. Weighting 11 tonnes, it had a crew of three, and was armed with a 76mm low-pressure L5A1 gun, and two M1919A4 machine guns. Nigeria acquired only 16 Saladin Mk.IIs – foremost because they proved both more expensive and less-well armoured than the French-made AMLs – but they played an important role and saw much action during the war of 1967-1970. Like the Panhards, all were left in their dark green colour overall, and only wore tactical unit insignia on the right front fender. (Artwork by David Bocquelet)

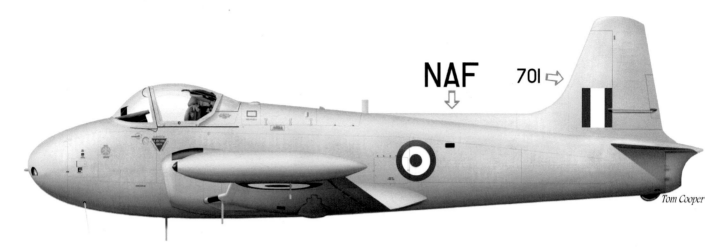

The Nigerian Air Force was established in 1964 from personnel trained in Ethiopia, Canada and India, and then worked-up with help of a large (West) German training team. Plans for the acquisition of Fiat G.91 and then Aermacchi MB.326 light strikers were abandoned when the country was subjected to an international arms embargo in 1967. The first jet fighters operated by the NAF thus became two British Aircraft Corporation Jet Provost armed trainers, donated by Sudan. Both arrived while still painted in high-speed silver overall: initially, they received Nigerian national markings only, before NAF titles and serials 701 and 702 were added. Subsequently, both were overpainted in matt green and earth brown on top surfaces and sides, and blue-grey on undersides: as well as retaining their national markings and serials, NAF701 also received a sort of unit insignia applied on the forward fuselage, the precise meaning of which remains unknown. (Artwork by Tom Cooper)

The first batch of eight MiG-17s to reach Nigeria were all old, second-hand MiG-17Fs (with afterburner) provided by Egypt. They were left in 'bare metal' or 'silver grey' overall (actually a double layer of clear lacquer mixed with 5-10% aluminium powder, applied over the natural metal surfaces), and were showing traces of former identification markings of the United Arab Republic Air Force, which included two black stripes on the rear fuselage and three around each wing tip. They had two double rails for Egyptian-made 88mm Sakr unguided rockets installed under each wing (the latter were rarely used during the civil war in Nigeria), and crudely applied black serials on the rear fuselage. Notably, their roundels and fin flashes were applied in green only, without any white in between. (Artwork by Tom Cooper)

The third type of jets to enter service with the NAF were eight Aero L-29 Delfin jet trainers acquired from Czechoslovakia, the first two of which arrived in August 1967 – together with a shipment of 600 OFAB-100 bombs and 600 LR-55 unguided rockets (fired from 10-round pods, one of which could be installed under each wing). Further deliveries in 1969 increased the number of L-29s to a total of 20 and brought additional ammunition to Nigeria. Initially, NAF L-29s were left in their bare metal overall colour (the same two layers of clear lacquer mixed with 5-10% aluminium powder as with the MiG 17s), but by late 1967 all were painted in dark beige overall, with their noses, wing- and fin-tips in dark olive green. National insignia was applied in the form of roundels, worn in six positions, while big black serials were applied on either side of the cockpit only. (Artwork by Tom Cooper)

Acquired as attrition replacements, the second batch of four MiG-17Fs arrived in Kano in April 1968, followed by another 16 in October and November of the same year. These aircraft received large roundels applied on their fins and – sometimes – roundels applied in four positions on the wings (a practice subsequently applied as standard on all Nigerian MiGs). Because of repeated Biafran air raids on their bases, many of the Nigerian MiG-17s were camouflaged in whatever green colour was available, but most often in the shade known as 'jungle dark green' (FS34227; inset shows the same aircraft after the green colour was applied). Their primary armament included two 23mm and one 37mm internal cannon, and diverse bombs from 50 to 250kg. (Artwork by Tom Cooper)

The fourth and final batch of MiGs to reach Nigeria in October 1969 included eight ex-East German MiG-17s (without an afterburner and thus without a suffix in their designation). With this, the total number of MiG-17s delivered reached 41, of which some 37 actually entered service (a few were destroyed in Biafran raids immediately after their delivery). Former East German MiG-17s were all painted in dark olive green overall shortly after their arrival and assembly at Kano AB in October 1969. In addition to black serials, they received fin flashes in green only. The inset shows the markings and the fin flash of the MiG-17F serialled as NAF625: the font and size of the serial different from aircraft to aircraft. (Artwork by Tom Cooper)

Nigeria received four Ilyushin Il-28 light bombers from Egyptian stocks in February 1968 and two from the former Soviet Union in April 1969. All received disruptive camouflage patterns applied in very different colours, including dark sand or light earth, and diverse shades of green. Most received the service title 'NAF' in black on the forward fuselage, but none can be definitely confirmed as also having its full serial (the range of which should have been NAF801 to NAF806) applied. The insets show their usual weapons – the same as used on Nigerian MiG-17/17Fs (which usually carried them instead of drop tanks) – including (from left to right) Soviet- and Czechoslovak-made FAB-250M46, FAB-100 (or OFAB-100) and FAB-50 general purpose- and incendiary bombs. (Artwork by Tom Cooper)

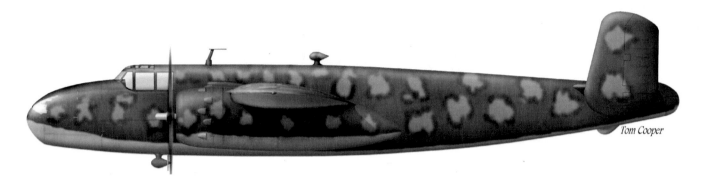

As well as the two well-known Douglas B-26 Invaders, the Biafrans also acquired two less-well-known North American B-25J Mitchell light bombers of Second World War-fame. They arrived in the territory in October 1967, but both were effectively lost only a few weeks later, after an air strike on Calabar airfield on 2 December. Both may have received four or five machine guns installed into the nose, and a camouflage pattern as shown here: consisting of olive green or dark blue, with grey-green or olive green spots softly outlined in black, on upper surfaces and sides. Undersurfaces were painted either in light grey or light blue. (Artwork by Tom Cooper)

Although acquired from French scrap dealers in late 1967, the 12 T-6Gs acquired by the Biafrans took much too long to reach their destination. They were overhauled in Lisbon in Portugal, and then flown into the territory in small batches. Indeed, only four are known to have been actually delivered to the Biafrans. (Artwork by Tom Cooper)

Thanks to efforts of the famous Swedish aviator Count Gustav von Rosen, a total of nine MFI-9B Minicos reached Biafra. All were painted in gloss olive green and black – applied by brush – on top surfaces and sides, and light grey on undersurfaces: the pattern differed from aircraft to aircraft. The first batch is known to have received consecutive serials from BB101 to BB105; the four aircraft of the second batch should have been serialled as BB903, BB905, BB907 and BB909, but it remains unclear if any actually received such markings. Some received small Biafran flags on the fuselage side, others a roundel instead. Their sole armament consisted of French-made pods for 68mm unguided rockets, one of which was installed under each wing. (Artwork by Tom Cooper)

Nigerian troops fire their 105mm pack howitizer onto Biafran positions.

Count von Rosen (right) helps a technician attach a rocket pod to a Malmo Flygindustri MFI-9B light military training aircraft operated by the Biafran Air Force. MFI-9B-pilots claimed no fewer than 11 enemy aircraft as destroyed on the ground, including 3 Il-28s, 4 MiG-17s, 2 Canberras, one Siddeley Heron and one C-46. Obviously, much of this was an exaggeration (for example, the NAF never operated any Canberras), but their operations did attract much publicity, which was one of von Rosen's objectives. *Source Albert Grandolini Collection*

MiG-17F NAF625 at Benin City in early 1969. It belonged to a large batch of MiGs delivered to Nigeria in the autumn of 1968. Most MiG-17Fs looked like this – 'natural metal overall' (painted in clear lacquer with 5% aluminium powder).
Source Keith E. Sissons via Albert Grandolini

NAF612 seen at Enugu in 1969. Of interest are traces of the identification stripes around the rear fuselage, peculiar to the United Arab Republic Air Force (official title of the Egyptian Air Force from 1958 until 1972). This was probably one of the few ex-Egyptian aircraft donated to Nigeria by Egypt (though delivered by the Soviets). Notable is the application of a large roundel (including white fields) on the fin: only four aircraft are known to have received national markings applied in this fashion. Source *Keith E. Sissons via Albert Grandolini*

NAF 615 preparing for take-off at Enugu in 1969. Again, 'standard' fin flash, but very small roundel between the title and serial, applied in green only (no white fields).
Source Keith E. Sissons via Albert Grandolini

Although all were flown and serviced by Egyptian crews detached to the NAF, each of Nigeria's Il-28s was camouflaged in different fashion: this one received a randomly applied camouflage pattern in green and black. The serial is unreadable – as usual.
Source Keith E. Sissons via Albert Grandolini

NAF 624 preparing for a combat sortie in front of NAF612, at Enugu in 1969. *Source John Fricker Collection via Simon Watson*

Two MiG-17s rolling for take-off from Enugu in 1969. NAF612 appears to be on the right. *Source Keith E. Sissons via Albert Grandolini*

Biafran flag. The colours represented peace, unity and freedom with the eleven rays of the sun representing the eleven Biafran provinces.

Biafran £1 bank note. *Source nairaland.com*

Lockheed L-1049G Super Constellation, Biafran government AN0417398. *Source Pedro Aragão*

Framed by the wing of C-124C 52-1004, this aircraft was operated on mercy missions by the International Red Cross during the Biafran conflict. *Source Mike Freer*

Lockheed L-1049G Super Constellation, Biafran government AN0684219. *Source Pedro Aragão*

MSN 16657 International Red Cross, Balair Pima, ex-USAF AS 52-2626 – Biafra, 1970. *Source Eric Salard*

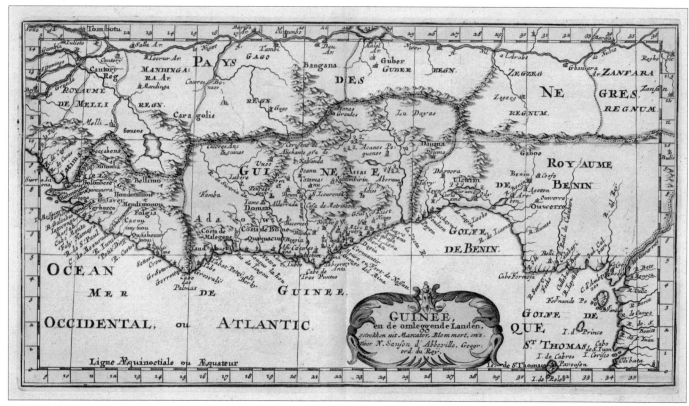

Map of the African Gold and Slave coast, c.1705. *Source Nicolas Sanson d'Abbeville*

Nigeria. *Source UN*

Biafran troops at Aba in September 1968 bang tin plates and shout to try and create the impression that their trenches are well defended. The fact that only one soldier has a rifle clearly demonstrates the sorry reality. *Source Private Collection*

military strategy.* That the Nigerians did succeed in occupying Bonny Island in a swift and relatively smooth operation tends to suggest that the Biafrans should have been aware of the potential and should have acted to forestall it, since this first beachhead on the coast of Biafra probably did more to set the stage for the fall of the rebel republic than any other single action of the war.

The landing operation was led by Colonel Benjamin Adekunle, commanding the Lagos Garrison Organization (LGO), renamed 3 Infantry Division. Adekunle was a field commander of fairly mixed reputation who was known by his men as the Black Scorpion, which was a suitably aggressive and fearsome *nom de guerre* for a commander with a reputation for individuality, iron control and a tendency, if pressed, for maverick and sometimes costly action.† Overall command of the operation up until the point that troops were landed and had occupied the island lay in the hands of Nigerian naval commander, Captain Nelson Soroh.

The naval operation was surprisingly complex. In total eleven ships were made available for the operation, only one of which, the NNS *Nigeria*, was a full-sized, all-purpose frigate, with the

remainder being a collection of seaward-defence boats, one survey boat, one landing craft and two merchant vessels. The main landing force comprised the brigade-strength LGO made up of three battalions, the 6th, 7th and 8th. The plan, in simple terms, envisaged a beach landing in several rapid manoeuvres with the objective of quickly dominating the island. The assault began on 26 July, and although it devolved into a chaotic and bloody land and sea battle, it was over relatively quickly with the effective eviction of Biafran forces from the island. The landing force was led by 6th Battalion, which took the bulk of casualties and handled most of the heavy combat, and 7th Battalion, which was later left to secure and garrison the island while the remainder of the force was withdrawn to Escravos, a point to the west of the Niger Delta in mid-western territory.

With the concurrent actions underway in the west and the north of Biafra, the commencement of operations in the south represented a third major offensive both for the Nigerians to mount and for the Biafrans to contain. The objective was obviously the complete encirclement of the breakaway republic with a view to compressing it into an enclave and, once again, limiting its practical viability to the extent that it would simply implode.

As something of a foreword to the commencement of what would be codenamed Operation Tiger Claw – the initial targeting of Calabar and surrounding centres as a precursor to further movement inland – the disappointment registered by the Nigerians that their slow chipping away of territory, and the isolation of Biafra from the outside world, did not immediately succeed in bringing down the rebellion can be blamed on none but

---

* Biafran intelligence on a certain level was improved by the numbers of Igbo living in the federal region, but ground-level tactical intelligence always remained slim.

† Adekunle was a somewhat unlikely figure for an aggressive fighting commander. He was short, wiry and curious in appearance – with large and mobile hands and a peculiarly animated and theatrical manner and an oddly high-pitched voice. Contemporary descriptions paint a picture of a disagreeable man conscious of an unprepossessing appearance and attempting, somewhat in the classic 'small man' manner, to compensate for this with loquacity, opinion and bombast.

Biafran casualties are evacuated by canoe during heavy fighting in June 1968. *Source Private Collection*

A severely wounded Biafran soldier waits at a primitive first aid station after being evacuated from the front. *Source Peter Obe*

Colonel Benjamin Adekunle, commander of the federal 3rd Marine Commando Division. *Source Private Collection*

Colonel Adekunle, goes through his plans for an offensive with his staff officers. *Source Peter Obe*

Major-General Yakubu Gowon, at Dodan barracks, informs reporters at a press conference that the war will be over in four to eight weeks, 13 September 1968.

the Nigerians themselves. Such had been the blatant victimization and the institutional genocide directed at easterners within the federation in years past, coupled with the ongoing verbiage of extermination that accompanied Nigerian operations, most of which were littered with blatant human rights abuses and multiple atrocities against civilians, that the general Biafran population during the early phases of the conflict saw no alternative to fighting other than the complete extermination of their race.

The Biafrans as a consequence threw disproportionate energy into limiting the inevitable Nigerian advance from what was clearly a game-changing toehold on the southern coast. It is worth pointing out that although many pro-Biafran observers at the time were wont to dismiss the catastrophic potential of the loss of Bonny Island to the republic, Forsyth being principal among them, from a military perspective the loss of Bonny Island represented nothing less than a new paradigm, particularly as it was accompanied in the same phase of the war by the loss of Enugu and the eviction of Biafran forces from the mid-west, followed by the eventual and inevitable loss of Onitsha.

At the head of operations in the south was, once again, the highly ambitious and aggressive Colonel Adekunle, now in command of a division comprising, in part, six battalions of what he had himself renamed the 3rd Marine Commando Division, in celebration of the amphibious assault, along with a variety of additional units.[*] Relative quiet settled on the northern and western fronts and for a brief and glorious season the Black Scorpion found himself in command of the most robust formation of the Nigerian Army in the most important theatre of the war. Significant infusions of manpower and ordnance, alongside the provision of technical expertise from various sources, most notably the British, gave Adekunle the technical and moral impetus to believe that he had it within his grasp to end the war almost single-handedly.

Calabar, defended by the Biafran 9 Division, fell on 18 October, a full three months after the fall of Bonny Island, which gives some indication of how effective the Biafran defence proved to be. The effect, however, was to seal the Biafran border with Cameroon and further isolate the dwindling republic, effectively completing the encirclement.

Thereafter Adekunle's division plunged westward, securing

---

[*] The 3rd Marine Commando 'Division' was in fact a regular army formation with some amphibious capabilities as part of their operational remit. Since most of their listed and recorded engagements were conventional combat operations, they were never formally designated as special forces. The amphibious capability of the force was provided mainly by outside advisers.

Nigerian troops fight from a flooded trench armed with G3 assault rifles. *Source Peter Obe*

first the town or Oron on the west bank of the Cross River, more or less adjacent to Calabar, doing so using the expertise of British amphibious experts, before then moving quickly to secure the adjacent provinces of Uyo, Anang and Aba. Thereafter, a brigade was despatched north to seize the towns of Afikpo and Obubra on the west bank of the Cross River, thus setting the stage for a major push against Port Harcourt, the next major strategic point in the southern sector and the last remaining major urban centre in Biafran hands after the fall of Eungu, Onitsha and Calabar.*

By the summer of 1968, Adekunle's division had bloated to a strength of over 25,000 men, including the vital logistical capability to handle the many amphibious operations demanded by the terrain and topographical circumstances of the south, which was provided by foreign, mainly British technical experts seconded to the Nigerian army in increasing numbers during this period. By the end of April 1968, Adekunle had crossed another significant river obstacle, the Imo River, at a point just forty miles east of Port Harcourt. Here a significant beachhead was defended against heavy Biafran defensive assaults as a rapid build-up of force was undertaken, before the first move against Port Harcourt in the closing days of April 1968 began.

The advance was made on three fronts: northward along the Imo River, centrally through Bori and in the west from Ika waterside to the southeast of the city, and Bodo West. The Biafrans fell back steadily, conceding Port Harcourt on 18 May 1968, as advancing Nigerian units cautiously entered the city. The Nigerians occupied the town with Biafran units in close attendance – with the anomaly of each side for some time occupying opposing ends of the airport runway.

Here, through August 1968, the two sides clung to their static positions and took stock. The capture of Port Harcourt and the effective encirclement of Biafra had achieved the major preliminary Nigerian objective, but the killing blow remained to be delivered, and it was this that the Black Scorpion, flush with success, and enamoured with his own abilities and the invincibility of his division, felt that he was uniquely poised to deliver.

While regrouping in Port Harcourt, Adekunle began privately to form an audacious and personally aggrandizing plan to complete the invasion of the south by seizing in quick succession the cities of Owerri, Aba and Umuahia, arranged in a triangular configuration in the south–central region of Nigeria, and in real terms the last substantive strategic region still held by the Biafrans.[†] This, informally codenamed Operation OAU – Owerri, Aba and Umuahia – was premised on an overestimation of both his own prowess as a military commander and the fighting capability of his division, coupled with an underestimation of the capacity for resistance on the part of the Biafrans who occupied an unpredictably fluid tactical hinterland that tended to be informed by the availability and supply at any given time of weapons,

---

* The Cross River is the main river of eastern Nigeria. It links with the Calabar River about 20 miles inland from the ocean, in a maze of swamps, inlets and tributaries, Calabar itself being just upstream of the confluence.

† Umuahia was the birthplace of the first military leader of Nigeria, Major-General Johnson Thomas Umunnakwe Aguiyi-Ironsi.

Biafran troops armed with VZ-58 assault rifles in trenches opposite Nigerian positions. *Source Peter Obe*

ammunition and ordnance. Up until that point Biafran resupply was available only via a tenuous air corridor maintained between Portugal and Biafra that was itself dependent on the continued ability of aircraft to penetrate the blockade and bring supplies into the constricting enclave.

In this regard it is incidental, but also extremely important, to make note of the fact that the comprehensive blockade of Biafra had begun to result in widespread hunger and malnutrition. The presence of large numbers of refugees prior to the outbreak of war had been exacerbated by huge numbers of internally displaced people and the concentration of the population of the breakaway republic into an ever-decreasing area of land.

It is here that we enter into what is perhaps the most controversial aspect of the war. While the subject of the airlift and the use of starvation as a weapon of war will be discussed in greater detail in a succeeding chapter, this was nonetheless an important pillar of the Nigerian strategy. As the war entered its last and most desperate phase, much thought and energy was applied on the Nigerian side to limiting the ability of the Biafrans to import food and arms, and the cat-and-mouse game played by the International Committee of the Red Cross and various other organizations to break the blockade and to land sufficient quantities of food and armaments

in the country to maintain some sort of viability in the resistance.

After the fall of Calabar and Port Harcourt, this international air operation became dependent on the viability of a single, improvised airport located in the east–central quarter of a shrinking Biafra. Uli, or Uli-Ihiala airport (codenamed Annabelle), was actually not an airport at all, but a 6,500-foot section of blacktop roadway lying between the towns of Owerri and Ihiala. This improvised runway had been widened slightly, and given a supplement of 90 feet of wing space added by clearing the bush on either side, and a parallel taxiway.

Knocking Uli airport out of commission became a major tactical objective for the Nigerians, and keeping it viable a matter of basic survival for the Biafrans. It was targeted with tremendous tenacity by the Nigerian Air Force, periodically coming within artillery range of Nigerian lines, and of course physically reaching and occupying this vital strategic installation, as humble as it was, informed much of Colonel Benjamin Adekunle's strategic planning as he pondered Operation OAU.

Any reading of the history of the Nigerian Civil War can hardly fail to leave a reader perplexed at the level of military incompetence that characterized operations on both sides from the onset of hostilities, with the Biafran armed forces displaying only one characteristic not also evident on the Nigerian side, and that was profound gallantry under incredibly trying physical circumstances, and against a catastrophic imbalance in arms, training, manpower and international assistance. Lamentable standards of discipline existed on both sides, and both sides perpetrated atrocities and abuses against one another, with the Nigerians making no excuses, or attempting in any meaningful way to cover up the wholesale targeting of civilians, both on the ground and from the air, and politically with the use of hunger as a weapon of war.

It was an ugly, scrappy, ill-mannered affair that displayed high levels of dilettantism, and not withstanding occasional flourishes of brilliant leadership, in general a damaging disconnect between high command and both division- and brigade-level operations on the ground, and to a large extent at a battalion and company level too. Troops on the whole were hastily recruited and superficially trained, and given free licence to treat the countryside and population as they chose. Individual interest tended to supersede tactics, and units and commanders were very often diverted from wider strategic objectives by abandoning offensives in favour of looting.* Heavy ammunition expenditure and generally poor fire drill resulted in a recorded total of 60 million rounds of 7.62mm ammunition being expended, with a similarly astronomical torrent of artillery, grenades, rockets, mortars and other infantry support ordnance.

Probably the best example of this sort of individualism and general disregard for overall command and strategy was the Black Scorpion himself. Adekunle was promoted to full colonel after the successful Bonny landing, after which he was awarded command of a cobbled-together 3 Infantry Division that was responsible for much of the action that followed. Although never a properly designated or trained special force formation, 3 Infantry Division did undertake some amphibious operations, and had some amphibious capability which, as mentioned, prompted Adekunle to rename it the 3rd Marine Commando Division after neither seeking nor being granted approval from army HQ.

Adekunle, however, overconfident and sufficiently removed from his central command to enjoy an almost total scope of autonomy in the southern theatre, recognized that, with the loss of Calabar and Port Harcourt and the steady if frequently ineffective pressure being applied on the Biafrans from the west and northwest by the federal 2 Division, and from the north by 1 Division, the opportunity lay within his grasp to bring matters to a quick and clean conclusion by the rapid seizure of the

remaining cities of Owerri, Aba and the new Biafran capital of Umuahia, all arranged in a triangular formation to the northeast of Port Harcourt, accessible by an excellent and widespread road network. This he had informally codenamed Operation OAU which he intended to hand to General Gowon as a gift on the eighth anniversary of independence from Britain scheduled for 1 October 1968.

In July that year, Adekunle began drawing up plans in earnest, predicting that upon the launch, Operation OAU would yield success in under two weeks. His plan in essence was to secure the small market town of Aba as something of a side operation by isolating the town and starving it into submission, while more or less at the same time advancing on the much larger centre of Owerri, in part the capital of Biafra after the fall of Enugu, using a simple double-envelopment strategy along three axes assigned to the 14, 15 and 16 Brigades of the 3rd Marine Commando Division.

Very simply, 16 Brigade would surge forward and penetrate Owerri at the centre, relying on 14 Brigade on the right and 15 Brigade on the left to protect its flanks, completing the envelopment once Owerri had been taken, thus preventing the deployment of reinforcements and any chance of a recapture. Simple indeed. In the meanwhile, an additional objective of 15 Brigade would be the capture of the town of Oguta, 15 miles or so northwest of Owerri, which would have placed the vital strategic airstrip of Uli within fairly easy artillery range, and in theory within a hair's breadth of capture. This, of course, bearing in mind that Uli was by then Biafra's sole supply lifeline, would have brought the war to a speedy and satisfactory conclusion.

Such was the plan, one of countless such military stratagems that failed upon deployment to survive contact with the enemy. The peripheral target of Aba was taken relatively easily after heavy shelling and an ugly infantry assault which resulted, on 14 September, in a Biafran withdrawal. Two days later, supported by armoured vehicles, mortars and artillery, 16 Brigade punched its way into Owerri, taking substantive control of the city on 18 September.

On the left flank, however, 15 Brigade had very quickly become bogged down against surprisingly determined Biafran resistance. This Adekunle had not anticipated, which of course he should have, not least because defence of this sector was vital if Uli airport was to remain viable and operational, so naturally the Biafrans would divert resources to this region. But another, perhaps justifiably unpredictable reason for the unexpected ferocity of the Biafran response was the abrupt infusion of French military supplies at precisely this moment.

Interestingly, the French under Charles de Gaulle were openly supportive of Biafra, going so far as explicitly to state that diplomatic recognition of Biafra had never been overtly taken off the table. This was a position very much at variance with other western powers at that time, particularly Britain, which supported the federal government both diplomatically and militarily, primarily, one supposes, for the purpose of not endangering British investments, but also, arguably, as the most sensible

---

* It is worth noting here that the Nigerian Army did not see significant action after the civil war of 1967–70 until ECOMOG (Economic Community of West African States Monitoring Group) was founded in 1990 as a vehicle to intervene in the Liberian civil war. ECOMOG was the child of ECOWAS (Economic Community of West African States), and although confined largely to Anglophone West African states, it was dominated by Nigeria. The Nigerian Army almost immediately abandoned its mandate to impose peace in Liberia and quickly became simply another armed faction. Local Liberians branded ECOMOG Every-car-and-moving-object-gone. Bearing in mind the lawless and corrupt nature of Liberia at that time, for Nigeria to stand out in quite this way, the levels of looting, privateering and general corruption must have been astronomical.

Nigerian troops with the body of a mercenary killed during an attack on the town of Calabar and which they had recently captured from the Biafrans. *Source Peter Obe*

strategy for preserving Nigeria and bringing the whole unpleasant business to a speedy end.*

Be that as it may, French arms shipments into Biafra began more or less at the moment when Operation OAU was launched. These involved air shipments organized by the mercurial and ever-shady French 'Secretary-General of the Franco-African Community', Jacques Foccart. Under the general umbrella of Operation Mabel, this in simple terms involved the transfer to Biafra of obsolete French weapon stocks from both Gabon and Côte d'Ivoire, which the French then replenished as part of recognized multilateral defence treaties established between various African Francophone countries and the French government under the terms of independence from France.†

Incidentally both Côte d'Ivoire and Gabon, along with Haiti, Tanzania and Zambia, were the only countries ever to offer recognition to Biafra, and indeed it was to Côte d'Ivoire that

---

* It is probably worth pointing out that the French were ever alert to an opportunity to thumb their noses at British overseas policy in Africa, in part for reasons of competition for influence in the region, a region where France has always been active, but possibly also for the sake of the enmities that have historically plagued the two nations. The French were never particularly squeamish about breaking Rhodesian sanctions, and did so against British diplomatic protests quite often.

† Jacques Foccart (31 August 1913–19 March 1997) was a chief adviser to the government of France on African policy as well as the co-founder of the *Gaullist Service d'Action Civique* (SAC) in 1959 with Charles Pasqua, which specialized in covert operations in Africa.

Ojukwu fled upon the collapse of Biafra. It is perhaps worth noting here that Uganda, under the leadership of Milton Obote, also came very close to recognizing Biafra, but backtracked only when Uganda was chosen as the venue for abortive peace talks between Nigeria and Biafra in May 1968.[21]

As something of a footnote to the diplomatic process, which was very much part of the strategy of both sides, the dynamic of recognition for Biafra in Africa was an interesting one. Apart from Rhodesia and South Africa, whose recognition at that time might not have been particularly desirable, the four main continental participants where Côte d'Ivoire and Gabon, and Tanzania and Zambia, two Francophone and two Anglophone territories; effectively two capitalist and two socialist systems, which tended to politically obfuscate the lines of an intricate neo-colonialist plot, which the OAU, to this day, retains as its most voluble strategy in dealing with outside pressure.

These recognitions, however, did serve to split the cohesion of the OAU but, in the case of Tanzania, recognition had much to do with the tremendous moral weight brought to bear on the debate by the doyen of the African community at the time, Tanzanian President Julius Nyerere. Nyerere's comments on the matter are quite revealing. "The breakup of Nigeria is a terrible thing," he wrote, "but it is less terrible than that cruel war."[22] Nyerere's decision to offer Tanzanian diplomatic recognition to Biafra was clearly not taken in support of the secession, but in the hope of bringing an early end to the war. Kenneth Kaunda of Zambia, a friend and confidante of Nyerere's, followed suit for much the same reason, hoping to strengthen Biafra's position at the forthcoming peace talks in Uganda. The two Francophone recognitions were primarily in support of the French position, and in an effort, one supposes, to bring Nigeria closer to the French sphere of influence.

To quote British journalist John de St Jorre: "The Kampala peace talks opened in the third week of May [1968] in a cloying atmosphere of mutual suspicion and mistrust."[23]

Quite so. Against a backdrop of the fall of Port Harcourt, and negotiating only under regional and international pressure, the federal delegation obviously had very little interest in reaching a settlement, and instead offered the Biafrans what were in effect terms of surrender. The Biafrans, on the other hand, flush with their recent diplomatic recognitions, were participating in the talks in the expectation of a flood of follow-on international recognition, and so held out for a ceasefire, an end to the blockade and the withdrawal of all troops to pre-war positions.

However, the Nigerians had by then overrun more than half of Biafra, were in occupation of all her major cities, industrial centres and sea ports, and so sensed, quite justifiably, that with a fair wind behind them, victory was imminent. As a consequence there was absolutely no incentive at that point to agree to the terms of a ceasefire and a general withdrawal. The opposing positions of the two sides illustrated nothing so clearly as the fact that neither side was particularly serious about a formula for peace. And so after six days the conference broke up under a mood of general acrimony, with both sides returning, with some optimism, to the business of war.

Renewed French support was responsible for much of this Biafran optimisim, and in collaboration with the French ministries of defence and foreign affairs, Jacques Foccart also made use of Ivory Coast, Gabon, and the Portuguese island of São Tomé as staging and resupply points for gun-running to Biafra, all with the full connivance of the French Secret Service. However, following aggressive diplomatic representations from Nigeria, Fernando Po (now Equatorial Guinea), and Cameroun (renamed the Republic of Cameroon in 1972) refused to cooperate with Foccart. Indeed, none of Nigeria's Francophone neighbours – Benin, Cameroun, Chad and Niger – ever supported Biafra.

In the meanwhile, the net result of Adekunle's audacious advance under the planning of Operation OAU was that he successfully took and held both Aba and Owerri, but then proceeded to make two crucial mistakes that neutralized much of this initial accomplishment. The first was to neglect to secure and patrol his supply lines from Port Harcourt to Owerri, which in fact had been a key tactical failing on the part of federal forces from the

General Olusegun Obasanjo, seen here with President Jimmy Carter during arrival ceremonies for the latter's state visit to Nigeria. *Source U.S. National Archives and Records Administration*

onset. Secondly, he neglected to drive what reserve forces he had – 13 and 18 Brigades of the 3rd Marine Commando Division – toward securing his control of Owerri, and thereafter capturing the town of Oguta, which would have placed Uli airstrip within his reach, without doubt the decisive card in the pack.

Instead Adekunle deployed those forces in a long-range and unsupported assault on the heavily defended centre of Umuahia, resulting in a punishing 14-day small-arms and artillery battle amid the jungles and minefields of this inhospitable region that achieved little more than the loss of upward of 15,000 federal troops and a disorganized withdrawal. Adekunle's signature failure in this operation, once again, had been to overextend and to fail to protect his lines of resupply and communications. The assault force was therefore adroitly cut off from the rear within a few miles of Umuahia, with the result that, by 7 October, six days after the 1 October independence day anniversary, the division had lost virtually all its troops and weapons.

A retreat to Port Harcourt was ordered, leaving 16 Brigade in occupation in Owerri, but isolated and trapped within a gradually constricting encirclement.

This was yet another catastrophic reverse for the forces of the Nigerian federation that altered the overall trajectory of the war not one iota, but did at least result in due course in the removal of the Black Scorpion from his place at the command of the southern theatre. Adekunle was relieved of his command on 16 May 1969 and replaced on 16 May by Colonel Olusegun Obasanjo, who moved immediately to restore the confidence of a depleted and demoralized division, and to prepare the ground for what would indeed be the defining and concluding phase of the war.

CHAPTER SEVEN:
ANNABELLE, MERCENARIES AND THE BIAFRAN AIRLIFT

All is fair in war, and starvation is one of the weapons of war.
I don't see why we should feed our enemies fat
in order for them to fight harder.
　　　　　　– Chief Obafemi Awolowo,
　　　　　　Nigerian Minister of Finance, 28 July 1969

The issue of starvation as a tactic of war, both directly by the federal government in terms of the intended effect of the blockade, and as a tool of propaganda as applied by the Biafran government, was, as it remains today, one of the most controversial issues of the entire episode. Millions of words have been written, years of academic time and labour applied and monumental amounts of verbiage deployed in order to sound the depths of this iconic, but also deeply deplorable aspect of the war.

There are two key factors to be considered here. Firstly, the comprehensive encirclement and increasing constriction of Biafra as the war progressed, and the sheer numbers of internally displaced, which rendered some sort of humanitarian disaster inevitable; and secondly, the fact that the treatment of the eastern population in general, and Igbo in particular, during the coups of 1966, alongside the atrocities committed by federal forces in occupied areas of the east and the threatening verbiage that continued to emanate from federal sources, tended to imply to the defenders of Biafra, that they were facing the stark choice of fight or face genocide. This, if nothing else, was an enormous incentive to retain Biafran resistance long after any practical hope of victory had evaporated. Clear evidence of this is that those fleeing the fighting tended to flee deeper into Biafra rather than out of it, which under normal circumstances would have been counter-intuitive, but clearly not in this case.

Most of those affected by hunger were, of course, children, and in respect of the fact that this was one of the first wars to be fought under the scrutiny of international television and press coverage, the images of Biafran children, skin pitched over protruding bones, bellies distended from Kwashiorkor, and dying in astronomical numbers dismayed overseas audiences and introduced a very ticklish public relations dilemma for western governments attempting to maintain a clear policy in defence of their economic interests and to some extent of Nigerian territorial sovereignty, and for the most part in support of the stated Organization of African Unity position.

Legitimate efforts by foreign governments and aid establishments to deal with this crisis ran up against resistance from both the federal and the Biafran governments. The federal government insisted that all aid operations within Biafra be coordinated from Lagos, and that all aid deliveries and shipments be routed through Nigeria, which

Refugee camp victims of the Gowon–Awolowo 'starvation is a legitimate weapon of war' doctrine.
Source magazine.biafranigeriaworld.com

Starvation as a weapon of war.

A group of French doctors and journalists created *Médecins Sans Frontières* (MSF) or Doctors Without Borders in the wake of the war and accompanying famine in Biafra, Nigeria. *Source MSF*

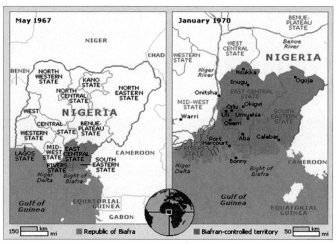

The gradual constriction of Biafran-controlled territory between May 1967 and January 1970. *Source igbofocus.com*

under the strict diplomatic rules of fair play was difficult to argue against because Biafra essentially remained unrecognized internationally, and so was therefore still theoretically part of greater Nigeria. Biafrans, on the other hand, claimed that food and aid shipments delivered through Nigeria, and there had been a few of these, had been laced with cyanide and could not be trusted.

There can also be no doubt that the ghastly imagery that daily saturated newspapers, magazines and television screens across the western world served the purpose of the Biafran high command, who made shameless use of these images for general propaganda purposes, but also in an attempt to tip the diplomatic balance toward recognition by the key global powers that would have quite reasonably resulted in a general recognition of Biafra. This strategy, although it ultimately failed, came reasonably close on a number of occasions to succeeding, certainly in regard to the potential for French recognition.

However, concerned international parties, non-governmental parties in the main, were faced for the first time in modern history, but certainly not the last, with the conundrum of trying to negotiate for space and opportunity to dispense food and humanitarian aid to where it was needed most against the entrenched resistance of both warring parties, each blaming the other for the deadlock. An interesting comment is attributed to then United States Secretary of State, Dean Rusk, echoing some of the frustrations felt at the time:

We [the United States] were concerned about food supplies for the Biafrans; we were ready to put in large amounts of food ourselves from our own stocks and were prepared to divert food ships going to other countries to Biafra. But the leaders of the two sides in Nigeria never could get together on the ground rules for furnishing food to the Biafrans, so the problem was not the availability of food but the ability to get it to those who were hungry.[24]

In the same interview, Secretary Rusk added for the record that: "Colonel Ojukwu, the leader of the Biafran forces, has to carry

a heavy share of the responsibility for the deaths by starvation in Biafra because he too was very difficult about the ground rules for getting the food in."

But then it must also be borne in mind that, given that the use of starvation was a clearly understood, and even defended policy of the federal government and a tactic of the federal armed forces, then it fairly stands to reason that no agreement or concession that Ojukwu might have made to facilitate the movement of aid into Biafra with the cooperation of Lagos would have worked anyway, and one need only examine very superficially an ocean of available documentation pertaining to negotiations with the federal government to conclude that obstructionism lay at the root of federal strategy, and that was that.

In the face of this inability of the more orthodox organizations like the International Committee of the Red Cross (ICRC) and the United Nations High Commission for Refugees (UNHCR) to make any meaningful headway, the operation to provide relief for Biafra was taken over by a far more informal operation known as the Biafran Airlift, a bizarre mixture of philanthropy and privateering which, quite interestingly, some writers and commentators, not least among them John de St Jorre, lump in with his general assessment of the mercenary activities associated with the Nigerian Civil War.

By the end of 1968, as military pressure from the south was beginning to gather momentum, and ongoing pressure in the west and the north was continuing to compact the Biafran population into an ever-diminishing liberated zone, an estimated minimum of 1,000 Biafran children were reported to be dying daily from malnutrition and associated disease.[*] Two Christian organizations – Caritas and the World Council of Churches – began purchasing large quantities of food and contracting space on aircraft bringing in arms shipments into Biafra to also bring in food.

Worth mentioning is the fact that these aircraft were owned by a German-American mercenary pilot by the name of Heinrich Wartski, also known as Henry, or Hank Wharton, who ran a conspicuously maverick airlift into Biafra known informally as Biafra Airways, operating out of Lisbon in Portugal. Thus Wharton ran an extremely lucrative gun-running operation into Biafra utilizing three aging Lockheed Super-Constellations, and flying almost entirely upon the goodwill of the Portuguese, embarking usually from Lisbon, and encompassing both Bissau in Portuguese Guinea and the well-placed Portuguese island of São Tomé, which lies nestled in the armpit of Africa, no more than 200 miles from the coast of Nigeria. Shipments were landed at the by now-iconic Uli airport, codenamed Annabelle, and for the year or more that followed, the busiest airport in Africa, handling at times upward of 50 flights a day.[†]

Soon afterward the International Committee of the Red Cross also began contracting space on Wharton's aircraft to ship food

---

[*] There have been many variations on this figure, and being that it was at that time such a volatile political issue, this is not surprising.

[†] Uli airport was initially improvised as a quick alternative to Port Harcourt, which was taken by federal forces in the middle of May 1968.

Nigerian troops wearing a mixture of steel helmets and berets are all armed with British-supplied Stirling sub-machine guns.
Source Private Collection

into Biafra, while at the same time attempting to negotiate with the federal military government right of access for daylight flights on its own behalf, using its own aircraft and crews. Needless to say these efforts proved fruitless.

As 1968 progressed, the humanitarian situation in Biafra worsened, in particular after the early successes scored by the Black Scorpion and his rampaging 3rd Marine Commando Division pressing up from the south, sending fresh waves of refugees north into a diminishing Biafra. Soon there was aggressive jockeying for space on Wharton's flights between opposing relief organizations, each of which in due course purchased their own aircraft, and began flying relief shipments out of São Tomé where food had

begun arriving in an earlier expectation of an agreement to land shipments and transport them by river into Biafra, an agreement which, of course, was never ratified.

The main problem for relief organizations lay in the fact that Hank Wharton was understandably reluctant to concede an extremely profitable monopoly on covert flights into Biafra, refusing to divulge the vital landing codes necessary to access Uli airport which, of course, operated under stringent security thanks to determined efforts by the federal military government to shut it down. The Biafrans were also reluctant to do anything to offend Wharton because at that point he represented the only meaningful link to the outside world, most importantly for arms shipments, which obviously superseded Ojukwu's interest in food aid.

The International Committee of the Red Cross eventually managed to secure these vital codes, which were immediately passed on to the various churches. This then opened the corridor for the first relief flights from São Tomé on the part of what then became Joint Church Aid, known also as Jesus Christ Airlines, and from the Spanish island of Fernando Po under the auspices of the ICRC.* Initially there was great reluctance on the part of relief pilots and crews to brave somewhat theoretical Nigerian anti-aircraft fire, until in August 1968 Swedish humanitarian and long-time mercenary pilot, Count Carl Gustaf Ericsson von Rosen, flew in a Douglas DC-7 at extreme low level, landing successfully at Uli airport, after which the floodgates opened and the iconic Biafran Airlift began.

A great deal of myth and lore has been attached to the Biafran Airlift, and this is probably for very good reason. The operation represented a strange symbiosis between humanitarians and mercenaries in the prosecution of an undertaking quite often blamed for a prolongation of the war. The funding and practical organization of the airlift lay in the hands of the various church organizations, with some being more prominent than others, while the practical business of flying was undertaken by a handful of highly paid maverick airmen from a variety of quarters and backgrounds. There were men prepared, at no insignificant risk, to fly nightly into an African war zone, under the threat of patrolling federal aircraft and anti-aircraft fire, to land on a widened stretch of blacktop road in the midst of the jungle, sometimes twice a night, sometimes more, in order to unload a mixed cargo of food and weapons, mainly the former, but quite often the latter, all in the interests of keeping this implausible separatist state alive just a little longer than practically feasible.

The aircraft used in the operation were mostly aging multi-prop airliners and transporters such as Douglas DC-3s, DC-4s, DC-6s and DC-7s, some smaller Avro Ansons, and the iconic and elegant triple-tailed Lockheed L-1049 Super Constellations. The flights were seen internationally as illicit, and certainly they were regarded as such by the federal military government, so for the most part, registration markings on aircraft were either removed or obscured. Most of these aircraft had been purchased at knockdown prices following the increased introduction of passenger jetliners, rendering the old prop generation largely obsolete.

Flights were only undertaken at night in order to avoid both federal anti-aircraft emplacements and the threat of federal aircraft ever present in the skies above Uli. Another factor was that during the day the airport would have been too easy for Nigerian Air Force aircraft to locate and identify, and therefore relatively simple

Joint Church Aid. The Biafran Airlift began in 1968.

Count von Rosen's air force. *Source vebidoo.com*

Uli airport, a simple strip of blacktop.

to bomb. The landing area, as previously mentioned, was really little more than a widened section of the blacktop road running between Uli and Ihiala, with a certain amount of bush cleared on either side to accommodate the necessary wingspan. During daylight hours, therefore, the minimal fixtures could be disguised, after which it was practically invisible from the air. The landing lights were deployed for no longer than thirty seconds during

---

* Joint Church Aid was an alliance of various church organizations, including, inter alia, American Jewish Emergency Effort for Biafran Relief, Canairrelief (an NGO organized by the Presbyterian Church of Canada and Oxfam Canada), Caritas, Das Diakonische Werk (a German church group), Holy Ghost Airline (run by the Irish Catholic Holy Ghost Fathers, Africa Concern), Nordchurchaid (an *ad hoc* organization of Protestant churches from Denmark, Finland, Norway, and Sweden), Oxfam, Save the Children Fund, UNICEF and the World Council of Churches.

incoming night landings, which could number anything up to 20 a night, after which they were hastily extinguished before circling Nigerian bombers could get a fix.

The airport was consistently targeted by federal bombers, but it was never put out of action. The strip was holed often, but relatively easily repaired. The big bomb that the Nigerians always hoped would put the airport out of action never hit its target.

Nonetheless, on the whole it was a hair-raising and technically extremely challenging operation to fly in and land at Uli under conditions of almost total darkness, and the presence alongside the old runway of 25 graves gives fair testimony to the risks.

Perhaps the most highly publicized incident came on 5 June 1968 with the shooting down of an ICRC DC-7 with the loss of all crew, after which the ICRC suspended all flights and re-entered negotiations with the federal military government for clearance to run daylight flights from within Nigeria, ultimately unsuccessfully.

The airlift, the largest of its type since the Berlin Airlift of 1948–9, lasted from the end of 1968 until the collapse of Biafra in January 1970 – incidentally, quite a number of the pilots who flew relief flights into Biafra had flown relief flights into Berlin during the Soviet bloackade. It reached its peak during 1969 when an average of 250 metric tons of food were flown in each night in an effort to sustain the estimated 1.5 to 2 million people, mainly children, who were dependent in one way or another on food aid. On average, although these figures are speculative, ten to 12 flights originated from São Tomé every night, six to eight from Fernando Po, and a further three to four from Libreville in Gabon. In total over 5,300 missions were flown, delivering some 60,000 tons of mixed cargo, mostly food, but also some medical and military supplies, and not infrequently fuel.

Historically, however, the Biafran Airlift is classified as a mercenary operation, which in practical terms it was. It was *ad hoc*, informal and only sparsely coordinated, with the bulk of the pilots involved being paid significantly more than their counterparts who flew under not dissimilar circumstances on the federal side.

Mercenary involvement on either side of the conflict fluctuated, but in very general terms there was a universal reluctance to make use of the soldier of fortune facility in the region so soon after the Congo Crisis, and the well-documented excesses and limitations that had come to light as a consequence of those events.* However, it was inescapable at the onset of hostilities that both sides lacked technical competence in many areas, particularly on the federal side, and in particular in the matter of air capability.

The Biafran Air Force, as improvised and ramshackle as it was during the opening phases of the war, was more than the Nigerians had, and it became necessary for the Nigerians to immediately rectify this as the first Biafran bombing raids began to be felt.

The Nigerian Air Force had been formally established on 18 April 1964, but at that point it only had transport capabilities, and even this was quite limited. Initially British, Rhodesian and South African pilots were hired at fairly standard commercial rates to fly converted DC-4s and DC-3s, and later British Jet Provosts.[25] Bi-lateral protocols, however, prohibited them from flying a number of Mikoyan-Gurevich MiG-17s that were presented to the Nigerian Air Force by the Soviet Union. At least 24 of these saw service during the conflict.

At a later point six Ilyushin Il-28 appeared in the skies over Biafra, flown largely by Egyptian and Czech pilots. These aircraft were delivered from Egypt, and for the most part were stationed at Calabar and Port Harcourt. The Ilyushins in particular became a highly discredited addition to the expanding federal air capability when during 1968 they were used to indiscriminately bomb targets in Biafra, both civilian and military, causing huge numbers of civilian casualties, and adding to the mounting humanitarian crisis that characterized the mid and latter phases of the war.

The Egyptian and Czech pilots were seconded to the Nigerian Air Force from their own respective air forces, so could not strictly speaking be described as mercenaries, and so they have tended to be described as foreign combatants, which is more accurate. The Egyptians, however, proved themselves to be of very limited value in combat conditions, firstly because they lacked night-flying capabilities and secondly because they appeared to suffer from an utter lack of motivation, causing them to eventually be replaced, on Soviet aircraft, despite official objections, with mercenary pilots who on the whole were a great deal more competent.

There were two factors, however, that frustrated the federal military government in regard to the use of mercenary pilots in a combat role. The two primary objectives of Nigerian air power were to take out Uli airport and to halt the relief and gun-running flights. These were achieving little else, it seemed to many, including numbers of foreign observers, than prolonging a war that could have been brought to a much cleaner conclusion without the involvement of a meddling corps of foreign do-gooders and privateers.

In regard to Uli airport, daytime sorties were of little value since the stretch of road that comprised the airport blended seamlessly with the rest of the road, and the airport building was indistinguishable under disguise from miles of similar roadside structures. At night however, as the flights were coming in, the landing lights were lit for 30-second snatches which served to alert circling bombers to the location of the airport and the proximity of relief flights. All that was then required was to plant a significantly large bomb on the tarmac to render the airport inoperable.

It has been speculated, however, that had the Nigerian government not opted for monthly payments into Swiss bank accounts, but instead offered mercenary pilots much larger sums based on results, Uli airport would have been rendered inoperable 18 months prior to the eventual end of the war.

In theory, taking out Uli airport should have been relatively easy, and it would have been, certainly, for competent pilots and

---

* There was also significant resistance to the overt use of mercenaries on the part of most established African governments which made up the membership of the Organization of African Unity. It is also fair to say that the employment of white mercenaries on the federal side amounted to an admission that the Nigerian military establishment was incapable of policing its own borders, which for a military structure as august as that of Nigeria – bearing in mind its British origins – was an admission indeed.

crew, but obviously there was a great deal of reluctance on the part of well-paid aircrews to deliver the killing blow that would put them out of work. Coupled with this there was also notable reluctance on the part of mercenary pilots to lock horns with fellow mercenary pilots, which would have broken a sacred code. Both federal aircraft and the relief flights were piloted by mercenaries, and only once was that code broken with the shooting down of the Swedish ICRC DC-7 by a British pilot flying a MiG-17. This incident not only scandalized the mercenary community, but it also created significant diplomatic and political fallout, causing the responsable pilot to suffer a nervous breakdown, and the incident was never repeated.

On the federal side, ground combat mercenaries were not used in any significant way at all. Technical assistance was provided on a military cooperation level in a number of instances, mainly by British personnel, and mainly in the matter of amphibious operations during the southern offensive to take Bonny Island, Calabar, Port Harcourt, and during Operation OAU.

The reasons for this wariness towards mercenary ground forces on the federal side were both military and diplomatic. In terms of ground operations, the federal military government suffered no shortage of manpower and ordnance, and if conspicuous tactical and command failures occurred, there is probably no reason to suppose that the infusion of numbers of mercenaries would have made much difference. There was also a profound distaste within the African political community, and federal authorities were obviously reluctant to bring upon themselves the criticism of other African countries. There was a desire in Africa to be seen to be capable of internal crisis management, and the ugly spectacle of highly paid non-Africans riding in to deal with internal security issues was never attractive.

On the Biafran side the sense that the rebel republic had been born with its back up against the wall rendered such diplomatic niceties a little less relevant, and mercenary combatants on the ground were a significant feature of the Biafran war strategy, for better or for worse. In the air, however, two notable characters contributed to the generally colourful pantheon of privateers in operation. Hank Wharton was probably the best-known transport operator active in Biafra, but a second individual by the name of Jack Malloch was also active in the skies over Biafra, and in fact arguably enjoyed a more diverse and prolonged career than Wharton, certainly in the African theatre.[*]

Malloch began his flying career as a fighter pilot with RAF 237 (Rhodesia) Squadron, alongside another notable Rhodesian personality, Ian Douglas Smith, rebel prime minister of Rhodesia who also flew over North Africa and Italy with 237 Squadron. After the war Malloch scraped together the funds to found an air freight company using war-surplus aircraft. After UDI in Rhodesia he was drawn into highly lucrative sanctions-busting operations from which he was able to assemble an enviable network of subterranean contacts across the continent, making

Jack Malloch.

American Hank Wharton, the legendary arms smuggler who used planes like the Lockheed Constellation on repeated missions to fly food to starving Biafrans through Nigerian air defences in 1968–9. *Source flycorvair.net*

him something of an obvious candidate to get involved in dissident transactions with the Biafran government.

According to southern African war historian Peter Stiff, Malloch's involvement in Biafra came about, at least in part, with the support and encouragement of the Rhodesian Central Intelligence Organization (CIO) in collaboration with the French external intelligence agency, the *Service de Documentation Extérieure et de Contre-Espionnage* (SDECE), primarily to ship arms into the

---

[*] Wharton and Malloch were by no means the only such operators. There were several others.

As TX166, this Anson joined the RAF in 1946 and served with various communications squadrons and station flights over the next 20 years. After demob, it arrived at Southend from RAF Shawbury on 24 July 1968 in full RAF Air Support Command markings for the British Historic Aircraft Museum, which was then in being at Southend. It quickly received the 'livery' shown here, including painting over the wingtop roundels with Red Cross marks and the BHAM logo on the fin. Whether there was ever a serious intent to use G-AWML on Biafra relief work is unclear.
Source British Historic Aircraft Museum

country via Libreville in Gabon, landing, along with the rest of the air-operation community, at Uli airport. These arms flights continued throughout 1968 and 1969, but Malloch was perhaps best known for transporting currency out of Biafra when the Nigerians opted for warfare by other means in an effort to bankrupt Biafra.

Because the two entities were essentially plugged into the same economic system, they shared a common currency at the outbreak of the war that was issued by the same central bank, and they continued to do so for quite some time afterward. The fact was not lost, however, on either side that there was great opportunity within this for mischief. Both governments sat on the fact until January 1968, when the federal government finally announced that the Nigerian pound would no longer be regarded as legal tender, after which the naira was introduced as the new federal currency. The effect of this was catastrophic on the Biafran economy.

In fact a comment by Biafran Major-General Alexander Madiebo, quoted in Jonathan Kirshner's book, *Currency and Coercion: The Political Economy of International Monetary Power*, fairly sums this fact up:

> The Biafran financial disaster, if not a total collapse as a result of the change in currency in January 1968, was the most important single reason why we lost the war. At the end of the financial chaos which followed in Biafra, we had lost over 50 million pounds which would have made a world of difference in our favour ... As a result of that fantastic loss, Biafra found it difficult to support her army at war.[26]

It became imperative to the Biafrans that they unload all remaining notes in their possession before the changeover rendered all of their held currency invalid. These were loaded onto any available aircraft and transported to Europe where they were taken by the Banque Rothschild in Paris at a discount of twelve shillings and sixpence per Nigerian pound. When the change occurred in January 1968, all remaining currency was immediately airlifted to Switzerland. Malloch's aircraft were involved in this emergency airlift, and the story is told of the impounding of one of Malloch's aircraft on the runway at Lome International Airport in Togo, packed to the rafters with newly minted Biafran currency, after which he, and another storied privateer gun-runner by the name of Alistair Wicks, and the entire crew were detained for five months in a Togolese prison, until their release could be negotiated by the Rhodesian CIO with the help of the French government. The seized aircraft was replaced soon afterward by the theft of a DC-7 which was known to be parked unattended at the far end of Lome airport, and which Malloch simply boarded and flew away.

Another notable character involved in the Biafran air war was Swedish Count Carl Gustaf Ericsson von Rosen, who has been mentioned earlier in the context of the relief operation, but who also, early in 1969, attempted to establish, or perhaps re-establish a Biafran air force almost single handedly in an operation that came to be known as Operation Biafran Babies.

Von Rosen was an interesting character. He was an authentic European nobleman with an insatiable thirst for adventure and a titanic social conscience. He flew on the Ethiopian side during the Second Italo-Abyssinian War, and then later during the Second

World War as the Russians were attempting to invade Finland. He quit his job as a commercial pilot with KLM and began flying bombing missions on behalf of the Finns. Later, when the Germans attacked the Netherlands, he flew covertly to Britain and attempted to gain entry into the RAF, which was refused on account of the fact that he was loosely related to German Luftwaffe supremo Hermann Göring. Von Rosen's Dutch wife joined the local resistance, meanwhile, but was arrested by the Gestapo and sent to Dachau in Germany, committing suicide in 1949. Carl Gustaf von Rosen went on flying for the Swedish Airline ABA from August 1940 until the end of the Second World War.

Another interesting fact about von Rosen was that he served with the United Nations in the Congo as the pilot for United Nations' Secretary General Dag Hammarskjöld, who famously was killed in an aircraft accident near Ndola in Northern Rhodesia. On that particular day von Rosen had been grounded by illness. Von Rosen was clearly therefore no stranger to Africa, and of course it had been him who had effectively kick-started the relief operation with the first daring low-level flight into Uli airport that encouraged the efforts of waves of mercenary pilots.

It later occurred to von Rosen, however, during a visit to Biafra during Christmas 1968 that "more than food, every priest, every doctor, every black and white was praying for arms and ammunition." Federal aircraft were bombing military and civilian targets in Biafra in an effort to compound the human suffering and break the back of the resistance. The question of how relevant shipping in relief food supplies was in the face of these ongoing catastrophic assaults, was being asked with increasing frequency. In order to survive Biafra first needed to be able to effectively defend itself. Von Rosen therefore embarked on a programme of intensive political lobbying for recognition and direct military support for Biafra, but when this failed he embarked on more direct action.

On behalf of the Biafran government, von Rosen secured six civilian, Swedish-built Malmö Flygindustri MFI-9 Junior aircraft. These were shipped to Libreville in Gabon, and there assembled, camouflaged and fitted with rocket pods. They were then flown to a secret bush airstrip were von Rosen, now aged 60, and a selected crew of two Swedish volunteers and four Biafran pilots, ran test flights before launching an attack against Port Harcourt directly from Gabon. Flying at treetop level, the improvised squadron attacked installations and an airfield in Port Harcourt, destroying strike aircraft and anti-aircraft positions, which probably achieved less in practical military terms than psychologically. The Nigerians were severely rattled by the attack, which was followed up in quick succession by similar raids launched against Benin and Enugu where several Russian-built aircraft were destroyed along with various oil and power installations in the mid-west. Thereafter these attacks continued somewhat haphazardly for the remainder of the war as more light aircraft were added to this rejuvenated Biafran Air Force, and as the Nigerians were challenged where they were most vulnerable – which was on the ground.

Operation Biafran Babies, however, although bold and innovative, was only partially successful in neutralizing the ability of the Nigerian Air Force to operate, doing little to impact the regularity of bombing attacks against civilian targets and the ongoing efforts to neutralize Uli airport. Von Rosen claimed inefficiency and corruption among Biafran officials for hampering his air effort against Nigerian economic and infrastructural targets, which he claimed would have ultimately forced the federal military government to sue for peace. Be that as it may, Operation Biafran Babies amounted to little more than another brave but somewhat quixotic effort to defend the indefensible, and again it probably achieved little more than to unnecessarily prolong the struggle to the detriment of those most affected. In his defence, however, von Rosen asked for and was paid nothing for his efforts, neither in this operation nor in his work with the relief flights.

The Biafran War was the second high-profile, post-independence conflict in Africa. The first was the Congo Crisis that followed immediately on from independence of what is today known as the Democratic Republic of Congo, which occurred on 30 June 1960. Poor planning on the part of the Belgian authorities, and an over-hasty departure all aided the plunge of this new nation state into mind-numbing levels of bloodshed and anarchy. The Congo Crisis also introduced the first foreign mercenaries into popular culture, somewhat glorifying the role of this grubby sub-culture and lionizing one or two individuals somewhat unjustly, creating reputations that have endured in popular culture ever since.

Mike Hoare, or 'Mad' Mike Hoare as he was perhaps more popularly known, was one of these. Hoare survived the Second World War as a relatively humble captain in the London Irish Rifles, building his reputation more on a keen nose for a market and a manufactured reputation than any particular field expertise. Others of a similar ilk were Bob Denard, a man with a somewhat wider resumé of conflicts than Mike Hoare, and another, Jean 'Black Jack' Shramme. Subsequent analysis of the contributions of mercenary forces to the outcomes and conduct of the Congo Crisis has left few of these men with an untainted reputation, and certainly without any notable record of achievement.

Early in the Biafran War, Mike Hoare put in a brief appearance with a proposition for a force of upward of 100 men to bolster the initially extremely feeble Biafran capability. Hoare was politely turned down, although ultimately numbers of mercenaries would be recruited by Biafra for the purpose of training and ground operations, although out of these only a handful proved viable, and of these even fewer distinguished themselves.

Throughout the separatist period, the Biafran government quite naturally lobbied assiduously for OAU recognition, and initially it was reluctant to offend the sensibilities of a number of key black African leaders who were keenly opposed to the use of white mercenaries anywhere in Africa. It was, however, French secret service chief and special adviser on African affairs to the French government who helped guide Ojukwu over his initial reluctance.

Jacques Foccart was one of the those enigmatic and enduringly interesting characters that littered the post-colonial African stage during that period. As *éminence grise* in charge of French

African affairs, he was actively involved in the various transitions to independence of all of the Francophone African countries, acting both overtly and covertly, and all the while accumulating a network of contacts that served him, in an informal advisory capacity, to the French presidency right up until his death in 1997.

As a consequence Foccart was extremely active on behalf of the French in Biafra, largely, one supposes, in order to carve out as large a slice out of Anglophone West Africa as possible, a region which in general terms the French regarded, in particular in the period immediately after independence, as being very much within their own sphere of influence. And in the absence of friends, not withstanding the Anglophone cultural slant of Biafra, Ojukwu was willing to entertain overtures from anywhere.

Although direct French military supplies to Biafra did not begin to arrive until later in the war, Foccart had been active since the onset of tension, prior to the outbreak of war, helping facilitate arms procurements for Biafra using his network of contacts and a number of French arms dealers.

Utilizing an ex-foreign legionnaire by the name of Roger Faulques, Foccart made the preliminary contacts for a contingent of French mercenaries to be formed. Faulques was a veteran of Indo-China, Algeria and the Congo, serving under French command, but later serving in Yemen and Biafra as a mercenary. On behalf of Biafra, however, he did little more than facilitate the recruitment of 100 Frenchmen for service in Biafra on a six-month contract. This contract, for which the Biafran government paid a reputed £100,000 in advance, saw the eventual arrival of only 49 mercenaries late in 1967.

The story that then follows is that this group was deployed in a somewhat brash and ill-planned operation to dislodge the Black Scorpion from Calabar, proving to those with Congo experience that Sandhurst-trained Nigerian officers were of an altogether higher calibre than the sparsely trained Congolese militias that they had encountered in an earlier war. The mercenaries were ambushed with five killed which, according to the rules of warfare acceptable to the average soldier of fortune, amounted to unacceptably high casualty ratios, and the detachment decamped soon afterward. After a certain amount of blame-exchanging and finger-pointing, the dust finally settled on the unsatisfactory affair with less than half of the men paid for completing less than six weeks of the six-month contract for which they had been paid.

It was Foccart, incidentally, who also leveraged South African support for Biafra by persuading Pretoria to provide the secessionists with arms and ammunition – South Africa, it must be remembered, was at that point building a substantial arms industry, ARMSCOR, which would in due course produce a range of conventional light and heavy weapons for its own use in South West Africa and Angola. South African arms supply was deemed desireable, largely, according to certain sources at least, because French pattern munitions did not fit British standard Biafran weapons. Ultimately South Africa provided Biafra with hundreds of tons of ordnance, as well, according to South African military historian and writer Al J. Venter, "as a squad or two of special force

German mercenary Rolf Steiner who fought in various West African hotspots including Biafra. This famous photo was taken by Italian war correspondent Romano Cagnoli. *Source Private Collection*

troops, all of it flown illegally across Nigeria's borders."[27]

Of all of the foreign mercenaries who served in Biafra, arguably the best known was a certain German ex-French Foreign Legionnaire by the name of Rolf Steiner. Steiner commanded, and in fact largely created, the Biafran Fourth Commando Brigade, sometimes described as the best unit in the army, commanding also as many as nine mercenaries of various nationalities.

There are a number of versions of Rolf Steiner's origins, including his own account of himself which is probably the least reliable, but nonetheless each tends to agree on certain facts. Born in 1933, Steiner joined the Hitler Youth in Germany – apparently at age 16; however, allowing for some combat experience before the end of the Second World War, as is claimed, simple mathematics proves this to be impossible. More likely was the version that after the war, and after service with the Hitler Youth, he decided to study for the priesthood at 16 with the goal of missionary work in Africa. Following an affair with a nun however, this career trajectory abruptly altered, at which point he decided at age 17 to join the French Foreign Legion. He saw action in Indo-China, losing the use of one lung – the question of whether this occured as a consequence of combat injury has never been adequately answered. He was a member of the Foreign Legion detachment that parachuted into the Suez in 1956, during the Suez crisis which saw French, British and Israeli forces attempting to seize control of the canal zone. He later served with the Legion in Algeria, marrying a *Pied-Noir*, or French Algerian, through whom he found himself

Biafran Army mercenary commanders plan an attack on Nigerian positions in November 1968. The three mercenaries are from left: Belgian Marc Goosens, South African 'Taffy' Williams and Corsican Armand Ianarelli. Goosens was killed leading a suicidal frontal assault a few minutes later where his death was filmed by a French film crew.
Source Private Collection

Belgian mercenary Marc Goosens who was interviewed shortly before his death in November 1968. Part of Goosens' motivation of fighting for the Biafrans was reported to be his hatred of the British government that he perceived was supporting the Nigerians.
Source Private Collection

allied with the anti-de Gaulle *Organization de l'Armée Secrète* (OAS), a French dissident paramilitary organization attempting to reverse moves toward Algerian independence from France. For this he was arrested and jailed for nine months, emerging from prison into civilian life. In 1967 however, he crossed paths with former Legion colleague Roger Faulques who was organizing on behalf of Jacques Foccart a mercenary force for the newly independent Republic of Biafra.

Linked to Steiner were a number of other foreign mercenaries who remained in the pan once the slurry of random individuals nefariously recruited had been washed out. Most commentators taking note of the Biafran conflict, and most particularly mercenary involvement, have tended to remark on the fact that Biafra had the effect of distilling a rare spirit of ideological commitment out of a handful of the men who came, and stayed. It is certainly not, and nor has it ever been, a mercenary trait to develop any personal commitment to the cause for which they fight, but Biafra was a rare case where this was not necessarily so.

Welsh South African Hugh 'Taffy' Williams was an example of this. Williams, a veteran of Mike Hoare's 5 Commando, is remembered as the bulletproof major for his habit of standing up

in the line of fire to encourage his troops in the thick of combat, acquiring a reputation for invincibility for which only *juju* could be responsible. Williams was the last mercenary to leave Biafra, serving ultimately two contracts and acquiring as he did a high level of respect for the troops that he commanded. Williams is quoted by Forsyth as commenting to the effect that: "I've seen a lot of Africans at war. But there's nobody to touch these people. Give me 10,000 Biafrans for six months, and we'll build an army that would be invincible on this continent. I've seen men die in this war who would have won the Victoria Cross in another context."[28]

Another of Roger Faulques' recruits was Marc Goosens, an ex-Belgian regular army officer who saw service in the Congo in 1964 as Belgium's chief adviser, assisting the *Armée Nationale Congolaise* (ANC), and who opted to return to Africa, this time to Biafra, purely on impulse, after a fight with his girlfriend. In November 1968, during a full-frontal attack against a Nigerian position in Onitsha, as part of Operation Hiroshima, Goosens was killed, and in one of the most dramatic moments of the war, and at great risk to themselves, a handful of Biafran soldiers were able to drag his considerable bulk back behind friendly lines.

The vehicle for the most successful mercenary activity in Biafra, however, was the Biafran 4 Commando Brigade, a unit devised, raised and trained largely by Rolf Steiner. The brigade was formed upon the order of Colonel Ojukwu, who specifically commissioned Steiner to undertake the task. Some 3,000 men were selected and divided into six small battalions, trained primarily by Steiner and Williams.[29]

Throughout its operational history, 4 Commando Brigade proved to be well commanded and tactically sound, although Steiner's personal Waterloo came with Operation Hiroshima, noted above, launched on 15 November 1968 in order to try and removed the Nigerian 2 Division from Onitsha, occupied in the aftermath of the disastrous misadventures following the Biafran invasion of the mid-west. Steiner ordered a surprisingly ill-conceived, full-frontal assault against Nigerian positions across an open area without artillery, air or fire support. The advancing Biafrans were decimated by Nigerian machine-gun fire, taking heavy casualties. Major Williams then ordered a unit under Goosens' command to attack a well-fortified Nigerian position, which resulted almost immediately in Goosens' death. By the abandonment of the operation on 29 November, almost half the brigade had been lost. Steiner seemed to suffer some sort of a nervous breakdown, lapsing into alternating bouts of paranoia and depression, all aggravated by heavy drinking.

On 6 December 1968 he was ordered to present himself in front of Colonel Ojukwu to be questioned on the events and abandonment of the operation. He arrived drunk, demanded a beer, which he then refused, claiming that the glass was warm, after which he berated Ojukwu's guard, attempted to slap Ojukwu,

and only narrowly avoided being shot when Ojukwu intervened.* Steiner was then escorted out in handcuffs and soon afterwards deported to Gabon in the company of five other mercenaries.

Major Williams thereafter was appointed commander of 4 Commando Brigade. Williams commanded the brigade in August 1968 during its attempts to halt the 3rd Marine Commando Division crossing the Imo River on its drive toward Port Harcourt. At that point the fighting core of the brigade had diminished to just 1,000 men, some fighting without ammunition. Following the arrest and expulsion of Colonel Rolf Steiner, Williams was thought to be the only European left serving with the Biafran Army. He left the territory shortly before the final collapse.

---

* Some accounts state it was Ojukwu who slapped Steiner, others that he was slapped by members of Ojukwu's guard.

New Biafran recruits march through their training ground singing patriotic songs. *Source Peter Obe*

CHAPTER EIGHT:
THE BEGINNING OF THE END

We shall all have to return to our provinces and villages.
We shall turn out and harass the enemy at every turn
and chase him out of our land.

– Major-General Emeka Ojukwu

When last we encountered the 3rd Marine Commando Division, it was mauled and demoralized in Port Harcourt with its 16 Brigade slowly being encircled in the city of Owerri. There the brigade was ordered to remain, by both divisional and army HQ, to defend the position to the last man, and, no doubt, defend the tattered prestige of the division itself, and its commander, Colonel Benjamin Adekunle.

The siege, and subsequent breakout of Owerri has arguably been one of the most studied and commented-upon episodes of the entire saga of the Nigerian Civil War. Colonel Benjamin Adekunle, the much-storied Black Scorpion, lost the equivalent of four or more battalions in his ill-conceived assault on Umuahia, with the result that 16 Brigade, under the command of Lieutenant-Colonel E. A. Etuk, was first encircled in the city of Owerri, and then later effectively besieged.

The wider situation in the shrinking territory of Biafra had by then also reached its most dramatic state. An estimated 10,000 people were dying daily from a combination of war, famine and regular and punitive bombings conducted against largely civilian and humanitarian targets. The shocking newsreel imagery seeping out into the wider world had finally prompted a freeze on arms sales to Nigeria, led by Czechoslovakia, Holland, Italy, France and Belgium, hoping ultimately to put enough pressure on the two sides to effect a ceasefire and begin peace negotiations. At the same time consignments of French weapons were beginning to arrive at Uli airport in regular deliveries. Temporarily, at least, this altered the battlefield dynamic, and the Nigerians, again very temporarily, were pushed onto the back foot.

The Biafran response to the Nigerian occupation of Owerri came in three phases, structured thus to accommodate the continuing poor supply, logistics and commissariat condition of the Biafran army, notwithstanding renewed arms shipments from France. These, incidentally, were not without problems, mainly in terms of the compatibility of ammunition with existing weapons' stocks.

The Biafran objective was simply to surround Owerri, cut it off and destroy the enemy within it. The first phase was simply to box the city in on all sides, taking care not to threaten the main Owerri–Port Harcourt road which it was thought would precipitate a premature abandoning of the city by the Nigerians. A successful completion of this phase would see Nigerian forces concentrated heavily within Owerri, after which the trap would be effectively closed by the seizure and securing of the 40-mile stretch of road linking Owerri with Port Harcourt. The third and final phase of the operation would be to pressure the encircled enemy inside Owerri in order either incrementally or dramatically to destroy him, while at the same time preventing him from breaking through southward toward Port Harcourt.

Even though the advantage was very much on the Biafran side, the plan had to be carefully and modestly rolled out. Biafran troops – hungry, barefoot in many cases, haphazardly armed – were expected to live off the land as much as possible, supplementing central supply of food, ammunition and general supplies with what they could forage, barter or steal.

Evidence of this creeping strategy began to be observed by the commander of 16 Brigade, Lieutenant-Colonel Etuk, as supply convoys plying the short distance between Port Harcourt and Owerri began increasingly to come under attack.

Each time he [the quarter-master] was coming back he would be ambushed. At times he escaped and a lot of goodies he collected from them would be shared by the rebels and the balance he would bring to me. So I reported back to my Divisional Commander, Adekunle. He didn't take the matter seriously and this continued until when supplies were no longer coming. I couldn't communicate with the outside since the battery of my radio was dead. I couldn't talk to anybody ...

By early November 1968, brigade detachments responsible for protecting the southern flank of Owerri where beginning to file daily radio reports indicating that the line of communication back to Port Harcourt was being increasingly threatened. However, divisional HQ remained unresponsive. An international military observer team, investigating Nigerian human rights' abuses, was briefly trapped in Owerri, eventually escorted back by a 120-man federal rifle company emergency-airlifted in from Port Harcourt.

To those within the city evidence of a gathering siege was inescapable, but the sense of urgency felt in Owerri could not be communicated to divisional HQ. This was perhaps largely because divisional HQ was embroiled within a typically Nigerian imbroglio, with brigade commanders fighting one another for access to ammunition and fresh troops, frequently filing false casualty, ammunition and battlefield reports with divisional HQ in order to gain an advantage over other brigades in the divisional supply chain.

By early in the new year, Biafran forces effectively controlled the main Owerri–Port Harcourt road, which completed the siege, successfully isolating 16 Brigade from its divisional HQ in Port

Harcourt. The evidence of this had been clear for some time, and really it can be seen as little other than naked face-saving and utter military incompetence on the part of the Nigerians that allowed the Biafrans, weakened as they were, to mount this operation over several months, and to bring about a successful conclusion, ultimately controlling over 20 miles of the 45 miles or so separating the two positions. Several hundred civilians were then deployed to render that stretch of road impassable, using mines, ditches and heavy trees felled across the road. Beginning on 8 January and lasting for several months, federal operations were launched up the road in an effort to clear it, operations that were significantly heavier and more costly to mount than a simple garrisoning of the route would have been, and which persisted until Owerri was eventually abandoned.

Phase three of the Biafran operation, however, floundered on sheer fatigue as a starving and exhausted army stumbled at the closing stages. On 15 January 1969, as the final phase to penetrate and destroy 16 Brigade in Owerri was mounted, Biafran troops were distracted by abandoned federal dumps of ammunition, food and clothing, and rather than maintain hot pursuit, hungry and ragged Biafran troops ignored their commanders, stopping short of their objectives, not only to eat, but also to change into newly captured boots and uniforms and to seize fresh weapons and ammu-

A Biafran soldier seen in 1969 poses in front of his comrades. He is armed with a Czech VZ58 assault rifle, one of the types of weapon imported just before the fighting broke out. His uniform has camouflage painted onto it by one of the uniform workshops producing clothing for the Biafrans. *Source Private Collection*

A Nigerian soldier armed with a Soviet-supplied AK-47 assault rifle examines the wreckage of a Biafran aircraft at Eket. *Source Peter Obe*

A Nigerian Ferret scout car crew shelters from the sun under the shade of a tree.
Source Private Collection

Lieutenant-Colonel Akin Akinrinade issues instructions during the battle for the oilfields at Owaza.
Source Peter Obe

nition. And while they were thus employed, a federal armored counter-attack swept them out of Owerri, back to the previous jump-off lines at their trenches on the perimeter.

From then on the situation devolved into an ebb and flow of probing attacks and counter-attacks, inconclusive on both sides, supported on the federal side by an ongoing offensive, including air strikes originating from AHQ. But by the end of January, having interpreted a muddle of Biafran propaganda on one hand, and the serious internal problem of false reporting by federal officers on the other, it became obvious to senior federal commanders in Lagos that Owerri had indeed been comprehensively encircled and besieged.

A certain amount of federal frustration at this impasse was registered through the indiscriminate deployment of L-29 Delphin armed jet trainers, MiG-17 fighters and IL-28 Ilyushin bombers in an attack that destroyed a village near Owerri, prompting renewed international press accusations that the Nigerian Air Force was indiscriminately bombing civilian targets while purportedly mounting military operations to relieve Owerri and take Umuahia.

The War was becoming more dogged and dirtier. Federal air attacks were stepped up and markets, hospitals churches, villages and other non-military targets were indiscriminately strafed and bombed, killing large numbers of civilians.[30]

In the meanwhile, a bout of internal soul-searching was underway in Lagos. The Nigerian Army Chief of Staff, Brigadier Hassan Usman Katsina, convened an urgent coordination and unity meeting of all federal divisional commanders in order to address critical rivalries that had begun to be felt between the various divisions. Each had begun to procure its own weapons independently from Europe, mounting surveillance at the port of Lagos in order to gain advance information on incoming arms shipments, even laying siege to the Shell depot at Apapa in order to secure fuel supplies for themselves. Weapons and fuel earmarked for other divisions were often hijacked and diverted.[31]

In the meanwhile, Lieutenant-Colonel Etuk was receiving orders to remain dug in and to hold his positions, while his concerns were mollified by assurances that a plan was being formulated at divisional HQ to relieve the beleaguered 16 Brigade. In fact there was very little afoot in this regard, and taking into account the extent of isolation, and the increasing danger of the brigade being overrun or forced to surrender, the only option available to the 3rd Marine Commando Division HQ in Port Harcourt was to arrange an airdrop to keep the brigade supplied. Without a resupply of water, ammunition, food rations, fuel, blankets, medical supplies, tents, spare parts and other essential equipment, morale within the brigade would very soon begin to crumble.

In the years since the war there has been a great deal of sneering criticism levelled at 3rd Marine Commando Division HQ's efforts to organize and sustain the airdrop, the facts of which have been cited as further evidence of general incompetence within the Nigerian armed forces. But in fact, bearing in mind the relative youth of the Nigerian Air Force, and its general equipment constraints, the effort to sustain the besieged brigade in Owerri stands as one of the more impressive logistical achievements of the war.

There has been some disagreement regarding the duration of the airdrop, with estimates ranging from six weeks to four months, but certainly at the very least it continued for six weeks, beginning 14 March and ending 19 April 1969. A revealing comment attributed to Lieutenant-Colonel Etuk is recorded by Nigerian military historian Doctor Nowa Omoigui, and published in a variety of forums:

> I got in touch with Adekunle and informed him that things were really bad. He told me to find a location for drops and to let him know. I never knew that as we were discussing, the rebels were picking up the message. So when that time came I told him I was going into the war zone and that there was going to be a big flame at so and so time and at so and so point. Of course, the rebels had got [the entire] message. Before that time the rebels had gone down and prepared a big flame. Adekunle rang me and said his pilot had taken off [from Port Harcourt] with all the goodies for my troops.
>
> The poor pilot sighted that first lighting point and dropped everything there while I sat waiting because I heard the plane when it took off hovering around. The pilot must have been a stupid man for I don't know whether he couldn't read his map to know exactly where I told my divisional commander things should be dropped. The whole stock was released to the rebels.

> When I got back to the radio and then called Adekunle and said I have not seen anything, he said, "You bastard son of a bitch, do you think you are the only commander I have?" The pilot went back and told him that he had delivered the goods and he said the pilot was there by him and he claimed to have dropped everything. Of course I replied that I saw nothing. That was the beginning of my woes, no supplies.[32]

Certainly the quality of air crew in the Nigerian Air Force was not excellent, but the Nigerian Air Force was just four years old, and was attempting to sustain an infantry brigade comprising initially 2,000 to 3,000 men under hostile fire, and with neither the air assets nor the trained personnel enjoyed by the combined organizations that were supplying Biafra in a similar way.

For example, no serious attempt can be made to mount an effective air bridge into an active war zone without, at the very least, large numbers of suitable aircraft, including, not just properly equipped transport aircraft, but also fighter escorts to protect against enemy aircraft, and bombers to contain enemy anti-aircraft ground fire. Also, a fine degree of logistical organization and coordination is a minimum requirement in a situation where all branches of the armed services are required to work under effective liaison and within a smooth working relationship.

Similar operational scenarios might arguably be the sieges of Dien Bien Phu and Khe Sanh during French and United States engagements in Vietnam. At Dien Bien Phu, a 16,500-man French garrison was besieged, while at Khe Sanh, about 7,000 United States Marines were closed off. In both cases, however, there were, initially at least, reasonably viable airfields into which supply aircraft could fly – albeit under hostile fire – in order to directly offload cargo. This remained the case throughout the siege of Khe Sanh, which lasted for 77 days, but not in the case of Dien Bien Phu, where the French were forced to rely on parachute drops, which was in fact precisely the scenario that from the very onset confronted planning staff at the 3rd Marine Commando Divisional HQ.

The Nigerian Air Force had neither the equipment, the manpower or the experience to effectively run an air operation of this complexity. When the civil war began in 1967, the NAF capability amount to a handful of piston-engine Piaggio P.149D trainer/liaison/utility aircraft and a few Dornier DO-27A general-purpose light transporters, alongside a couple of French Alouette III helicopters. When the first active forward operational base was established, this list grew to include not only a few Jet Provosts acquired from Sudan and Egypt, but also two Douglas DC-3 twin-engine 21-passenger aircraft seconded from Nigerian Airways.

The DC-3s had been adapted for offensive purposes by the addition of bomb racks and machine-gun mounts, and were in fairly constant demand for bombing, air patrol and casualty evacuation. This remained the case until they were supplemented by the addition of several larger DC-4s with a greater capacity and a longer range, as the NAF began to spread its assets to

A young Nigerian soldier involved in fighting for the oilfields at Owaza. *Source Peter Obe*

Battered Biafran POWs held by Nigerian guards for the camera. The guards are armed with World War II-era Sten sub-machine guns. *Source Peter Obe*

bases located at Calabar, Benin, Lagos and Enugu. It would seem that only a single DC-3 was diverted from operations over the Uli-Ihiala bombing patrol to attend to airlift duties over Owerri, supported by fighter jets and bombers that targeted Biafran positions around Owerri, but which did not appear to act in close support of airlift operations.

Bearing in mind the numbers involved, and the degree of mechanization of the besieged force in Owerri, the daily requirement for accurate airdrops, not including the quotient lost through wind variants, inaccuracy and liaison failures, of which there were many, would be upwards of 10,000lbs as a bare minimum, with 120,000lbs a more likely figure, taking into account all the variables.

With only one DC-3 aircraft available, with a maximum load capacity of 6,000lbs of cargo, anything up to 20 round-trip flights every day, in and out of potentially hostile Owerri airspace, would have been required to practically sustain the besieged force in a manner comparable with either Dien Bien Phu or Khe Sanh. Clearly the task was monumental.

And the result, not altogether surprisingly, was a bold effort and a fairly comprehensive failure that resulted in Biafran units gaining access to an estimated 50 per cent, but perhaps more, of all supplies destined for Owerri. Naturally in the aftermath blame flew in all directions, but a catalogue of failures can be recorded, among them the inexperience of the Nigerian Air Force, the lack of appropriate equipment and personnel, high-altitude drops and a signature lack of operational coordination between the Army and Air Force.

Not to be forgotten, or understated, must also be the cunning and resourcefulness of the Biafrans who recognized in this situation a potential bonanza. In this they were aided in no small part by the fact that ongoing attrition against the besieged brigade ensured that the area within Owerri under Nigerian control was small, and getting smaller. It was reported that any Biafran unit that wanted an airdrop simply had to clear a small area of land, spread out a white sheet and bounty would drop from the sky. According to Lieutenant-Colonel Etuk:

> They [NAF] used passenger aircraft to be dropping things – so you come and see another line of battle – when this plane started coming and hovering around town, the rebels were waiting – when they knew that the plane was there they would be waiting for any drop that came – so it was a battle for my troops to be able to collect these things and for the rebels too – so it was cross-fire. So this thing continued and continued; each time the plane took off [from Port Harcourt] everybody was ready. At times the pilot would come but because of the firing from the rebels he would go back with all the cargo. He couldn't come down nor could he even go within the level at which he should drop these things.[33]

Trapped in Owerri, none too confident in the quality of leadership and support at divisional HQ in Port Harcourt, and with stern orders to hold the position at all costs, Lieutenant-Colonel Etuk was faced with a very unpleasant conundrum. The United States Marines besieged at Khe Sanh a year earlier were in a position to reflect on the fact that the weight of the most powerful military organization ever known would be brought to bear in their support, but no such comfort existed in Owerri. At that moment meeting his fellow divisional commanders in Lagos, Colonel Adekunle very much played down the crisis in Owerri, instead concentrating his efforts on securing the task, for the second time, of taking Umuahia, this time in competition with Colonels Mohammed Shuwa and Ibrahim Haruna, who commanded the federal 1 and 2 Divisions respectively.

This determined quest for personal prestige ahead of the well-being of his troops is fairly indicative, not only of Adekunle himself, but the general standard of divisional leadership available to the federal armed forces at the time, and the degree to which competition and partisanship had begun to supersede unified command and control and shared objectives.

For example, if Adekunle had been fully focused on the plight of his besieged brigade in Owerri, his obvious course of action would have been to have urged army HQ to authorize a push by 1 Division south toward Owerri, supporting a push northwards by his own 3rd Marine Commando Division, under which conditions 16 Brigade would have been fairly easily relieved. The wider strategic value of this would have been to have effectively

divided Biafra into two, separating the capital of Umuahia from the all important Uli-Ihiala airfield, which would almost certainly have rendered further Biafran resistance pointless – although whether that would have immediately ended the war is debatable, but it certainly would have shortened it.

Instead, Colonel Shuwa, at the head of 1 Division, was ordered by army HQ, at that point not wholly aware of the extent of the crisis in Owerri, to take Umuahia, perceived then to be the last major pillar of Biafran resistance.

This left 16 Brigade very much alone, and Colonel Adekunle himself isolated, depressed and completely bereft of ideas. For Lieutenant-Colonel Etuk in the increasingly constricted operational space of Owerri, the situation was bleak indeed, and his options extremely limited. Initially, there had been an attempt to continue the original operation along its planned axis, which at the time would have relieved the brigades pinned down west of Umuahia, but this option was abandoned fairly quickly, after which it was either a case of hold out in Owerri or break out.

Etuk at least had the advantage of armoured capability, comprising a brace of British Ferret scout and reconnaissance vehicles, British Alvis Saracen armoured personnel carriers and Alvis Saladin armoured cars. Apart from the obvious advantage these offered in holding his static position, Etuk could also reasonably easily punch out of the encirclement if and when this became necessary.

Initially, of course, the 16 Brigade commander would have been reasonably confident of air support and effective aerial resupply, accompanied by the expectation that the brigade would be relieved in due course, or at least before the point that it would be facing surrender or destruction.

The Biafrans initially eschewed any temptation to assault the city directly, relying instead on general attrition using snipers, probing hit-and-run attacks and artillery when it was possible, all of which, although punishing, extremely effective and steadily diminishing enemy brigade numbers, did not ultimately provoke any moves toward a surrender.

Eventually, however, Biafran forces, by mid-April fully appraised of Etuk's hopeless situation, mounted a long-anticipated attack along multiple converging axes with full confidence that Etuk – by now desperately short of men and supplies – would be in no position to effectively retaliate. It was by then recognized by the Biafrans that their temporary capital Umuahia would fall sooner rather than later, and this reinvigorated Owerri offensive was really nothing more than desperate strategy on the part of the Biafran high command to seize something in compensation, or to in some way divert attention from the pressure building against the seat of government.

Biafran forces now concentrated on the outskirts of Owerri assumed a hostile attitude toward incoming relief flights, which, until then, they had not shot at thanks to the simple fact that they were arguably being resupplied more effectively than the trapped brigade. But the final flight, undertaken on April 19, 1969, was met with such concentrated ground fire that it returned to Port

Harcourt immediately, riddled with bullet holes. This would be the last effort divisional HQ would make to support or resupply the beleaguered brigade, by which time Biafran units had in any case penetrated deep enough into Owerri to be within shouting distance of Etuk's HQ.

This finally forced Etuk to make a choice between surrender, displacement or complete destruction. For months his diminishing brigade had endured repeated mortar and 105mm artillery barrages, ongoing firefights in and around a destroyed city, sniper attrition and gradual and morally debilitating diminution. It was time. With the fact now fully appreciated that the brigade had been abandoned, the decision was fairly easy for Colonel Etuk to make: to ignore the preposterous stand and fight directives issued by army and divisional HQs, and instead to exfiltrate the city to the south and make a dash for the safety of Port Harcourt.

According to Colonel Etuk:

> My decision to withdraw wasn't proper. The Army Headquarters should [ordinarily] give me the go-ahead but I did [without authority] and said let me be court-martialled when I am out with my troops. [If] I didn't do that, it would have meant complete elimination of the whole troops and that was what Ojukwu was waiting to do. If not through hunger it would have been through torture by whatever means he chose to use. But the Army Headquarters did little or nothing to get me as a Brigade Commander out of that place. What sort of battle organization is that? So I said to myself, "When I come out let them put me on trial." But they didn't do it; maybe they knew that that was the only way to save the few lives I was able to.[34]

In the predawn hours of April 25, 1969, three days after the successful federal capture of Umuahia, Lieutenant-Colonel Etuk led his diminished brigade out of Owerri via a disused diversionary route, avoiding the main road to Port Harcourt, thus limiting any likely Biafran response.* The besieging Biafrans offered limited response initially, allowing the armored column to get clear of the city before harassing attacks began. According to Biafran general and army commander, Alexander Madiebo:

> During the night of the 24 April the enemy began to move out of Owerri to the uncontrollable joy of all. Once out of town, a Biafran company was put on their trail to harass them and hasten the withdrawal. At Umuguma, the major battle began on the morning of the 25th and the enemy suffered

very heavy casualties indeed. Many vehicles carrying women, children and enemy casualties were allowed to proceed on their journey southwards unmolested. After 24 hours of heavy fighting, the enemy shifted further down to Avu, only to face another Biafran force waiting for them there. After barely four hours encounter[ed] at Avu, the enemy moved again further south to Ohoba and there linked up with his counterparts advancing from the south.[35]

The link-up of 16 Brigade with the rest of 3rd Marine Commando Division took place at a place called Ohoba, a tiny settlement on a nondescript section of forested road where today a commemorative artillery piece stands as a monument to an extraordinarily emotional moment in military history.† Notwithstanding a catalogue of blunders, incompetent command, criminal lapses in planning, political interference and a lamentable failure to perform, the emergence of the remnants of 16 Brigade from Owerri, in possession of their rifles and ordnance, ranked behind their commanding officers, and although thoroughly reduced, in formation, in uniform and on their feet, was a moment of heroic triumph.

There has never been an official casualty list published in relation to the siege and withdrawal from Owerri, but anecdotal sources tend to suggest that of the 3,000 or more troops that entered the city in September, 1968, only some 300 survived uninjured to rejoin their division. The consequences of the recapture of Owerri by the Biafrans was catastrophic on the morale of 3rd Marine Commando Division in particular, but on the Nigerian armed forces in general. It shattered the myth of the division and the reputation of its commander, both of which had been formed by the spectacular drive north from Bonny Island, culminating in the capture of Port Harcourt. A signal was sent to Nigeria and the wider world that there were still one or two stiff kicks yet left in the dying Biafran donkey, and of course Biafran morale, just weeks earlier staggering under the weight of inevitable defeat, now surged with renewed vigour.

Strategically the recapture of Owerri temporarily nullified the successful capture of Umuahia, creating a pivot for subsequent aggressive probes south toward Port Harcourt, but perhaps most importantly, it relieved pressure on the all important Uli-Ihaila airstrip.

On the Nigerian side, the most significant result of the disaster was the removal from his command of the Black Scorpion, Colonel Benjamin Adekunle. Adekunle was by then something of a spent force, emotionally exhausted, convinced he was being victimized by northern officers, and at the head of a division that desperately required the infusion of new leadership, new ideas and a revival of morale. As Biafran forces were regrouping and beginning to probe south, desertions from the ranks of 3rd Marine Commando Division were commonplace, not to mention self-inflicted wounds and a general lack of confidence in the war effort and the

---

* On 27 March 1969, in an operation codenamed Operation Leopard, and with the support of a squadron of armoured vehicles, artillery and engineers, five federal infantry battalions launched a comprehensive assault on Umuahia. NAF fighter-bombers later assisted in close air support, notwithstanding a number of deadly friendly-fire incidents. Once alerted to the objectives of the operation, Ojukwu attempted to mobilize troops and assets from other operational sectors, including Owerri, in order to shore up the defences of Umuahia, which stalled the Nigerian advance, but in two weeks of heavy fighting, failed to stop it. On 22 April, four days before the breakout from Owerri, the Nigerian 21st and 44th Battalions occupied Umuahia.

---

† An M2A1 105mm howitzer of United States manufacture, widely used in Africa at that time.

Nigerian troops pose for the camera near the end of the war with the man in the foreground armed with a German MG42 machine gun. Unlike the Biafrans, the belts of bullets draped around him show that the Nigerians rarely suffered shortages of ammunition. *Source Private Collection*

was an absolute public relations disaster. Against a torrent of international protest, the oil men were tried and found guilty of supporting the enemy.

The Biafran response to the international dismay was simply that: over the fates of 18 white men, Europe is moved, over the deaths of millions of blacks she has been supine. Where was the justice in that? Ultimately clemency was secured by a personal intercession by the pope. Late in June 1969, the 18 men were released and flown out of Biafra in the custody of diplomats from Côte d'Ivoire and Gabon.[36]

In the meanwhile. a radical overhaul of the senior divisional command of the federal army took place. It was publicly announced, on 12 May 1969, that Colonel Olusegun Obasanjo would replace Colonel Benjamin Adekunle as GOC 3rd Marine Commando. Four days later, on May 16, 1969, Obasanjo physically assumed command of the division in the field. The transfer had been delicate, however. Adekunle was a Yoruba, and there was a considerable Yoruba contingent in the 3rd Marine Commando Division so, as something of diversionary tactic to avoid any ethnic backlash upon his replacement, all of the senior divisional com-

leadership of both the division and the federal armed forces in general. A mood of disaffection and war weariness was growing in the country, and increasingly strident calls for a negotiated peace were being heard. It was vital that matters be turned around.

In the midst of all this, news broke that a Biafran commando operation had attacked an Italian-owned oil installation near the town of Kwale upon information that oil workers were feeding Nigerian forces sensitive information. Eleven workers were killed in the initial assault – ten Italian and one Jordanian – with a further 18 taken hostage. Fourteen of these were Italian, three were German and one Lebanese. This operation, ill-conceived at the very least,

manders were replaced at the same time.

Nonetheless, the transfer was effected under a cloud of bitterness and acrimony. Obasanjo and Adekunle despised one another. But interestingly, Obasango was an engineer and not a combat officer, which is either suggestive of his obvious abilities or the fact that there were very few unsullied commanders at that point for the army high command to choose from. He was 32 years old, and commanding upwards of 35,000 men.[*]

The end of the war came like a flash of tropical lighting momentarily

---

[*] Olusegun Obasanjo would in due course head the federal military government of Nigeria between 1976 and 1979.

CHAPTER NINE:
IN CLOSING

illuminating a half-remembered landscape and reimposing itself on the consciousness of a world ... It took everyone by surprise

– John de St Jorre

Remaining within Biafra throughout the three years of the war, working for the Biafran Political Orientation Committee, and helping to build and rebuild civil society in Biafra, Nigerian writer Chinua Achebe recognized the inevitable as the new year of 1970 dawned, commenting that, among other omens of change, the Harmattan season of that year was particularly harsh:

> I remember vividly the suffering of the people; everything seemed particularly bleak. The dry sandy air seemed to be an additional torment, delighting in covering the body with a layer of the Sahara desert's fine dust. Blown in from hundreds of miles away. This made it impossible for bare, weeping, vulnerable skin lesions to heal. It was particularly hard on the children. Looking around one could see a proud, devastated people.[37]

On the front line – there was of course no front line, the three Nigerian divisions were closing in on all sides – the sense of finality was no less acute. The recapture of Owerri by Biafran forces was quickly followed by a deep southward thrust toward Port Harcourt. The federal grip on Aba was slipping and federal morale was arguably at its lowest point since the start of the war. The tactical advantage at that point lay very much with the Biafrans who were occupying countryside between and behind federal positions, which created a long and indefensible federal line whose forward units then had to fall back.[38] There also appeared to be a curious sense within the Biafran high command that time was on their side. General Ojukwu stated publically, and rather brashly, that at that point Biafra was in a position to fight for another decade, speaking perhaps from a mood of temporary exuberance caused by the Biafran recapture of Owerri.

The initial six weeks of Colonel Obasanjo's command was therefore spent containing a Biafran advance on Aba, which commanded the Umuahia–Port Harcourt road, and was key to the recapture of Owerri, as well as rebuilding stocks of ammunition, straightening his line and touring front-line positions to shore up morale. Initially his strategic objective was first to retake Owerri, and then to proceed to take Oguta, before finally moving toward the all-important Uli airport, which had been, and which remained, the lynchpin of Biafran resistance. By November 1969, however, Nigerian reconnaissance probes had begun to reveal gaps in Biafran defences that convinced Obasanjo that a better option at that point would be to mount an advance on a broad front toward Umuahia in order to link up with 1 Division, effectively cutting what remained of Biafra in half, before then turning west and advancing on Uli, by which point it could fairly safely be surmised that Biafran resistance would crumble. This strategy was codenamed Operation Finishing Touch.

Operation Finishing Touch was launched on 22 December, and as predicted Biafran resistance began to crumble almost immediately. Once the 3rd Marine Commando Division had reclaimed Owerri and linked up with 1 Division in Umuahia, dissecting Biafra and isolating the all-important food-producing region of Arochukwu in the east, the writing was very much on the wall. By then Biafran units had already begun to disintegrate:

> Demoralised, disenchanted and distraught all at once, a large majority of our people, soldiers and civilians alike, had become altogether despondent about their future. Many of our soldiers, having discarded their personal weapons and shed their tattered uniforms, had taken to the bushes as deserters and stragglers. A handful of others, taking the line of least resistance, had ultimately defected to the enemy side.[39]

The relief effort flying into Uli airport also began to wind down as contact with air traffic control at Uli more or less ceased. On the evening of 9 January, 17 relief aircraft managed to land and unload, but the fall of Owerri the day before had more or less stamped the end of the enterprise, and soon afterwards ICRC and other relief personnel began to be pulled out of Biafra.

> ... suddenly Biafra's nerve cracked: doctors and nurses disappeared into the bush; the wounded dragged themselves out of their beds to follow them; soldiers went on a rampage of looting and, from all sides, people converged on Uli airfield.[40]

Obasanjo, in the meanwhile, reached Umuahia on Christmas Day, 1969, and without pausing to break his stride, he veered west toward Uli. Operation Tail Wind was launched on 7 January, and after a heavy aerial and artillery bombardment, Uli airport was finally captured on 1 January 1970.

For three days General Ojukwu sat in morbid conference with his cabinet and military advisers, slowly bending to the inevitable. And at 06h00, on 11 January 1970, a pre-recorded message was broadcast over Biafran radio announcing that Ojukwu would be leaving the People's Republic of Biafra in order to explore alternative options for peace. By then he had already fled the country, one of the last to leave via Uli airport, having already sent his family on ahead to Côte d'Ivoire.

The following day, Radio Biafra announced that the new Biafran leader, General Phillip Effiong, General Chief of Staff, vice-president, and current president, whom General Ojukwu had handed over to prior to his departure, would make a statement. In it Effiong called on the armed forces to lay down their weapons, and in a thinly disguised reference to the departed Ojukwu, commented, "those elements of the old regime who had made negotiation and reconciliation impossible have voluntarily removed themselves from our midst."[41] And after a brief recapitulation of the events of the three years past, he concluded with an appeal to the federal military government to respect a ceasefire.

The next day Obasanjo and Effiong met. After a few moments of cordial conversation, during which, according to Obasanjo, Effiong was lightly chided for placing preliminary conditions on surrender, the Biafran leader was told in a friendly but soldierly fashion that surrender would be complete and unconditional. And so it was. Effiong flew to Lagos a short while later, the surrender was announced soon afterwards, and on 15 January 1970, the formal surrender ceremony was held, and the Republic of Biafra ceased to be.

There was a sense almost of shock as the two sides parted, so unexpended when it came was the end. Perhaps in a way, like two brothers tearing each other's hair out, and then stepping back asking one another: "What on earth where we thinking?" An almost emotional flush of reconciliation consumed both sides as the 'One Nigeria' ideal became a reality, and determination to prove its worth, at least on the federal side, informed much of the immediate post-conflict verbiage. There was no sign of the genocide that the Igbo had so long feared, and in fact had ceased to really believe in toward the end of the war.

It was in the matter of aid, however, offers for which came rushing from

This Nigerian soldier had adopted the US soldier's practice in Vietnam of painting his nickname on the front of his steel helmet. His *nom de guerre* on the helmet was probably earned in the bitter fighting with the Biafrans. *Source John de St Jorre*

all quarters, that the western world was at last presented with an opportunity to salve the conscience that had tormented it for at least 18 months past. Not, though, aid from France, Portugal, South Africa or Rhodesia. In words not precisely spoken by the Nigerian leadership, but certainly passionately felt, these countries could go to hell. The ICRC, various Catholic organizations, and many serving Catholic individuals, were pressured to leave Nigeria, and did. Uli airport, that thorn in the paw of the federal government for so long, was bulldozed and torn up and scrubbed from the face of the earth. There was a sense, not unjustified, that without all of that do-gooder meddling, and the support of a handful of foreign powers, the war would have been bought to a much cleaner conclusion a great deal sooner. General Yakubu Gowon wrapped up this early response with a statement that no further interference by any foreign government or organization would be tolerated in the internal affairs of Nigeria. And there matters rested.

It is interesting, and instructive, to observe the concluding comments of British journalist John de St Jorre in his superb chronicle of the war, *The Brothers' War*, published in 1972, soon after the end of the affair, and obviously when it was still very much fresh in his mind. De St Jorre takes very much a journalist's view of the conflict, and in a crisply observed 400 pages, he chronicles much that defined and informed the war, without dwelling in unnecessary detail on campaigns, statistics and manoeuvres. His is arguably the finest and most comprehensive analysis of the episode to date.

Touring Biafra in the aftermath of the peace, de St Jorre made the observation that everywhere, and from every direction, columns of refugees were on the move, all returning home. The threat of genocide did not materialize, and nor was there any overtly retributive forum such as the Nuremberg trials. And of course the age was premature for such a thing as a Truth and Reconciliation Commission, such as served to help heal, or at least superficially scar over, many of the grosser wounds of South Africa's apartheid era, and which have also helped in more recent conflicts such as that in Sierra Leone, and to a lesser extent in Kenya, Ghana, Uganda and many non-African conflict zones.

De St Jorre also exploded some of the early myths of the conflict that arose both during the war and immediately afterwards, many of which still endure to this day. Genocidal levels of starvation did not exist.* The use of starvation as a tactic of war was not systematic. It occurred only as a by-product of the blockade, and certainly was never on the level that it was widely portrayed. Tens of thousands, perhaps even hundreds of thousand died from hunger- or malnutrition-related issues, but certainly not the millions often touted.

Chinua Achebe, commenting on the same period, makes the point that there was mass panic as the realization of defeat dawned on the surviving Biafrans, but in reality, by then, there were more Igbos living safely outside of the territory known as Biafra than inside it, and fears of genocide had been then largely dissipated – although, that is not to say that looting, rape and punitive killings did not take place. This was particularly true in the south where the 3rd Marine Commando Division remained in occupation, and these at times took place on a platoon and company level, but never battalion, and certainly not divisional. In fact, apparently, more striking was the image of soldiers who had been bitter enemies days before, embracing one another on the battlefield. One supposes that some of these had been comrades in the Nigerian army before the split, and many, of course, would be comrades again.

Myths also circulated as to why the Biafran military structure collapsed so suddenly, and so completely, after months and years of almost superhuman endurance. By the end of the war, the average Biafran soldier was better armed than at any time prior, and although in general terms all rank and file troops were undernourished, those on the front line were somewhat better fed, and moreover had access to what could be looted from the Nigerians. Two factors probably stand out as important, and these are morale and heavy equipment. The lessening of fears of genocide, and the gathering hopelessness of the wider situation, coupled with the fact that the Biafrans lacked artillery and armoured capacity to drive forward an offensive, contributed more significantly to the eventual collapse when it came than hunger and other more obvious factors.

There was also significant speculation and rumination on the hasty and sudden departure of the lynchpin of the entire episode, General Chukwuemeka Odumegwu Ojukwu. A residual bitterness lingers even to this day, several years after his death, at an act of naked self-preservation at the end of what some have categorized as a self-aggrandizing folly on a massive scale. "Whilst I live Biafra lives" was apparently Ojukwu's parting comment, and one is forced to ask oneself, so many years after the fact: who cares?

There can be no doubt that, bearing in mind the political mood of the times, and the unmistakable fact that the Igbo were very much on the receiving end of Eastern European-style pogroms, that the call for secession was not in any way unjustified. However, there has also been no shortage of exposure given to those voices within the governing establishment in Biafra who preached reconciliation and negotiation long before the end. There can be no doubt that once the inevitability of defeat had become apparent, that if Ojukwu's pathological unwillingness to concede had been curbed earlier, tens, if not hundreds of thousands of unnecessary deaths might have been avoided.

Ojukwu nonetheless occupies a unique place as a popular folk hero in Nigerian mythology, although his triumphant return to Nigeria after 13 years in exile was crowned with neither notable political achievement or office. He was briefly imprisoned alongside many others during the repressive years of military rule under Generals Ibrahim Babangida and Sani Abacha, and would later be instrumental in Nigeria's return to democracy. But beyond that Ojukwu remained a third-tier political figure in Nigeria at

---

* Genocide: the deliberate and systematic extermination of a national, racial, political, or cultural group.

best. On 26 November 2011, at the age of 78, Ojukwu died after a brief illness. His body was returned to Nigeria from the United Kingdom where he was afforded the highest military honours, and a lavish funeral parade held in Abuja. His body was interned in a newly built mausoleum in his family compound at Nnewi, in the heartland of what had once been Biafra. He remains a central figure in Igbo mythology.

In conclusion, the Biafran War, or the Nigerian Civil War, resulted in upward of 100,000 military casualties, and anywhere between 500,000 to 2 million Biafran civilians who died in one way or another as a consequence of the war. The latter figure varies wildly, depending who one acknowledges as the source, but what is inescapable is that a colossal price in human life and suffering was paid in pursuit of an ephemeral national unity that remains as ill-defined today as it was then.

Since the first words of this narrative belonged to Chinua Achebe, it seems fitting that the last words should too:

After a war life catches
desperately at passing
hints of normalcy like
vines entwining a hollow
twig; its famished roots
close on rubble and every
piece of broken glass.

A Nigerian soldier embraces a Biafran soldier at the surrender ceremony of the rebel army in January 1970. *Source Peter Obe*

Notes

1. Achebe, Chinua. *There Was a Country.* (The Penguin Press, New York, 2012) p. 43
2. *Times* (London). *Lady Lugard on Nigeria.* 2 March 1904, p. 12
3. *The Geographic Journal.* No. 1, Vol. XXIII, January 1904. Brig-Gen Sir Frederick D. Lugard, KCMG, CB, DSO, High Commissioner.
4. Arinze, Josh. *Moral Anguish:* Richard Nixon and the Challenge of Biafra. Kindle Edition.
5. Ibid.
6. Baxter, Peter. *Rhodesia: Last Outpost of the British Empire.* (Galago Press, Alberton, 2009) p. 192
7. Achebe, p. 74
8. Lalola Toyin, Heaton, Mathew, M. *A History of Nigeria.* (Cambridge University Press, 2008) p. 148
9. *The Trouble With Nigeria*, Achebe, Chinua. Quoted: Achebe, Chinua. *There Was a Country.* (The Penguin Press, New York, 2012) p. 76
10. Siollun, Max. *Oil, Politics and Violence: Nigeria's Military Coup Culture (1966-1976).* (Algora, New York 2009) p. 44
11. Forsyth, Frederick. *The Biafra Story: The Making of an African Legend.* (Pen & Sword, UK, 2013) p. 86
12. Leapman, Michael. *Independent.* Sunday, 4 January 1998
13. Mwakikagile, Godfrey. *Ethnic Politics in Kenya and Nigeria* (Nova Publishers, 2001) p. 55
14. Ibid. p. 56
15. Ibid.
16. Stiff, Peter. *The Silent War: South African Recce Operations 1969-1994.* (Galago Press, Johannesburg, 1999) p. 20
17. Forsyth, p. 116
18. de St Jorre, John. *The Nigerian Civil War* (Hodder & Stroughton, London, 1972)
19. Achebe, p. 129
20. Forsyth, p. 124
21. Mwakikagile, Godfrey. *Ethnic Politics in Kenya and Nigeria* (Nova Publishers, 2001) p. 55
22. Ibid, p. 178
23. de St Jorre, John. *The Brothers' War: Biafra and Nigeria* (Houghton Mifflin Co., Boston, 1972) p. 200
24. Rusk interview, 8 March 1970, p. 27
25. de St Jorre, John. *The Brothers' War: Biafra and Nigeria* (Houghton Mifflin Co., Boston, 1972) p. 315
26. Madiebo, Colonel Alexander A. *The Nigerian Revolution and the Biafran War.* Quoted: Kirshner Jonathan. *Currency and Coercion: The Political Economy of International Monetary Power.* (Princeton University Press, Princeton, 1995) p. 105
27. Venter, A.J. *War Dog: Fighting Other People's Wars: The Modern Mercenary in Combat.* (Casemate, Havertown, PA, 2006) p. 334
28. Forsyth, p. 113
29. Gould, Michael. *The Biafran War: The Struggle for Modern Nigeria.* (I.B. Taurus, London, 2012) p. 96
30. de St Jorre, John. *The Brothers' War: Biafra and Nigeria* (Houghton Mifflin Co., Boston, 1972) p. 290
31. Nowa Omoigui – dawodu.com
32. Ibid.
33. Ibid.
34. Ibid.
35. Madiebo, p. 351
36. Achebe, p. 220
37. Achebe, p. 222
38. Lliffe, John. *Obasanjo, Nigeria and the World.* (James Currey, Suffolk, UK, 2011) p. 28
39. Gbulic, Ben. *The Fall of Biafra.* (Enugu, 1989) pp. 55, 108-9
40. de St. Jorre, John. *The Brothers' War: Biafra and Nigeria* (Houghton Mifflin Co., Boston, 1972) pp. 396-7
41. Aka, Jubil. *Blacks' Greatest Homeland: Nigeria Is Born Again.* (IUniverse, 2006) p. 47

Peter Baxter is an author, amateur historian and African field, mountain and heritage travel guide. Born in Kenya and educated in Zimbabwe, he has lived and travelled over much of southern and central Africa. He has guided in all the major mountain ranges south of the equator, helping develop the concept of sustainable travel, and the touring of battlefield and heritage sites in East Africa. Peter lives in Oregon, USA, working on the marketing of African heritage travel as well as a variety of book projects. His interests include British Imperial history in Africa and the East Africa campaign of the First World War in particular. His first book was *Rhodesia: Last Outpost of the British Empire*, followed in 2014 by *Rhodesia Regiment 1899–1981*. Peter is a regular contributor to the Africa@War series.